Rooting Your Teen in the Faith

Rooting
Your Teen
in the Faith

Kim Cameron-Smith

Our Sunday Visitor
Huntington, Indiana

Nihil Obstat
Msgr. Michael Heintz, Ph.D.
Censor Librorum

Imprimatur
✠ Kevin C. Rhoades
Bishop of Fort Wayne–South Bend
November 28, 2022

The *Nihil Obstat* and *Imprimatur* are official declarations that a book is free from doctrinal or moral error. It is not implied that those who have granted the *Nihil Obstat* and *Imprimatur* agree with the contents, opinions, or statements expressed.

Our Sunday Visitor Publishing Division
Our Sunday Visitor, Inc.
200 Noll Plaza
Huntington, IN 46750
www.osv.com
1-800-348-2440

ISBN: 978-1-68192-931-6 (Inventory No. T2673)
1. RELIGION—Christian Living—Parenting.
2. RELIGION—Christian Living—Family & Relationships.
3. RELIGION—Christianity—Catholic.

eISBN: 978-1-68192-932-3
LCCN: 2022948024

Cover design: Tyler Ottinger
Cover art and Interior art: AdobeStock
Interior design: Amanda Falk

PRINTED IN THE UNITED STATES OF AMERICA

With gratitude to Greg and Lisa Popcak and Gordon Neufeld, grown-ups who helped me (mostly) grow up so I could help my children grow up.

Contents

Introduction: Becoming Your Teen's Shepherd   9

Lead

1   Gaining Insight into
    Your Teen's Faith Journey   29
2   Anchoring Your Teen in Love and Faith   59

Inspire

3   Questing with Your Teen on Mission   99
4   Forging a Faith Village for Your Teen   121

Free

5   Mentoring Your Teen in Discernment   145
6   Managing Challenges While
    Protecting Your Relationship   179

Transform

7   Toward Owned Faith   213
8   Your Faith Journey: Gaining Perspective   239

Conclusion: You're the Answer   251
Acknowledgments   255
Notes   257

Introduction
Becoming Your Teen's Shepherd

It is I; do not be afraid.
— JOHN 6:20

They try to warn you. When you're bleary-eyed after being awake all night with a baby or toddler, your mom, grandpa, or maybe an older friend says something like, "Well, enjoy it while you can because before you know it, she'll be grown up, and you'll miss these days." Blink, and here we are, years later, looking at our teenagers, wondering where the years went. You may also be wondering how you will navigate the challenges of the years ahead. You feel like you just got this parenting gig down, and now you're confronted with your teen's angst, pimples, and impulsiveness. As a Catholic parent, you're also worried about your teen's fragile faith, particularly in a world that is hostile to it.

I'm glad you're here. By the end of this book, I hope you'll feel inspired and equipped not only to survive the coming years but to strengthen your relationship with your teen and your teen's relationship with God. I have four children: one adult child, two teenagers, and a tween. It's true, I *do* miss the days when they were all little, back when our life seemed simple, and their problems and questions were easily addressed. But I am enjoying this stage of my mothering just as much, if not more. As my children grow up, I am privileged to witness them coming into their own, discovering their gifts, and considering their futures. Conversations with them about books, politics, and relationships are fascinating. I also get to sleep through the night, except maybe when the conversations have been a little *too* fascinating!

As a Catholic parent, the most important way I want to see my children come into their own is in their faith, and the most important conversations I have with them are about God and the Church. Ultimately, I want them to possess a bone-deep faith that animates their lives and forms their identities.

I'm a revert. I left the Church as an older teen out of ignorance and hard-heartedness. I lost the greatest treasure I ever had because I didn't understand it and because, quite frankly, I didn't want to understand it. Praise be to God, I returned to the Church in graduate school after many years of wandering and searching for a spiritual home. Some people might say it was the path I needed to take, but this is untrue. It was an unnecessary loss that I could have avoided if I had understood what was at stake. I want my children to know what is at stake. I want them to know what we believe as Catholics; I want them to experience the beauty of our liturgy and different prayer traditions; I want them to understand the reasons for the Church's moral and social teachings; I want them to know what God has in store for them on earth and in heaven.

Catholic parents, like all Christians, are called to spread the Gospel to the world. This is Christ's Great Commission to his Church, and it's as much our duty and privilege to take up this mission as it is the duty and privilege of priests and religious brothers and sisters. Parents have a heightened duty to ensure their children are catechized and formed spiritually, so their hearts might be prepared to respond to Christ's invitation to follow him. While the claims on our time and attention are dizzying, nothing is more important than transmitting the Catholic Faith to our children. Evangelizing our child is more important than his piano lessons, standardized test scores, or position on the baseball team.

Parents as Gardeners (and Shepherds)
In my first book, *Discipleship Parenting: Planting the Seeds of Faith*, I shared how parents can cultivate a fertile and healthy home environment where the seeds of a child's faith can germinate and take root rather than lie fallow. I talked about the importance of love, balance, empathy, playing together, and building a Catholic home culture, among other things. In this way, parents are gardeners, and our homes are protective greenhouses for the tender shoots of a child's faith. In that book, I also described parents as shepherds (yes, mixing my metaphors!), taking a gentle but confident lead, guiding children where they need to go while keeping them safe from harm.

That book did touch on many issues that you care about as the parent of a teenager, and I highly recommend it for understanding how our home environments and relationships with our children can create a rich soil in which the seeds of faith can thrive. I had not anticipated when writing that book that I would write a follow-up focusing on teenagers. But I've noticed something as I have led workshops and retreats for parents over the last few years. More than any other group, the parents of teens struggle to shepherd their children with confidence. They have the most questions and live with the greatest fears about their teenagers' faith lives. So, this book is for those parents.

If my first book was about planting the seeds of faith in rich and hospitable soil, this book is about providing the right kind of "faith fertilizer" when our child reaches adolescence. Surely, we continue doing many things, no matter our child's age. We continue loving them unconditionally and supporting them when they hit roadblocks. But we really can't nourish a teenager's faith in precisely the same way we do a young child's. Nor can we assume our teens are spiritually and morally mature enough to manage without us. A teenager lives in a kind of liminal space between childhood and adulthood. One minute she wants permission to drive our car into the city, then the next minute she needs our help with her algebra homework. Teenagers experience an inclination to separate from us in some ways, but they are not ready in most ways. They become more capable of thinking abstractly about the rituals, Scripture, and liturgical practices that have shaped their faith lives during childhood. Still, their faith questions are not always well-formed, informed, or sophisticated. These years are an exciting and dynamic stage of spiritual growth, but our teenage children continue to need the shepherding of wise adults.

You may be wondering whether you did enough "faith stuff" when your teen was younger or whether you know enough about the Faith to pass it on to your teen. Rest assured, none of us gets it entirely right; we all come to parenting with varying strengths and weaknesses and varying levels of energy and knowledge. Despite our imperfections, every parent has what it takes to raise a teenager whose faith grows robust and resilient, with deep roots, capable of surviving storms beyond the protection and safety of home. As you read this book, you'll become more confident that you can shepherd your wonderful, complicated teenager toward a path of continued growth in holiness and conviction, not just in the first few years after he leaves home but hopefully for his lifetime. We'll tease out some of the points I made about teenagers in *Discipleship Parenting*, providing greater context and practical direction. We'll learn more about adolescent faith development and how parents can facilitate opportunities and extend invitations to nourish their teens' Catholic identity and relationship with God.

Obstacles in the Field

If you want to stare into a chasm of futility and stay awake all night again like you did when your kids were babies, read statistics on the state of faith practice in young adults. The Fuller Youth Institute reports that 80% of teenagers involved in church activities say they plan to continue practicing their faith in college, but in follow-up interviews, nearly half of this 80% report that they struggle with or have lost their faith in college.[1] And these are kids who assumed they would remain faithful Christians! Young adults today are twice as likely to describe themselves as agnostic, atheist, or religiously unaffiliated than young adults thirty or forty years ago. These statistics are sobering for parents and youth leaders. Something has gone terribly wrong.

The explanations for this phenomenon are numerous and complex, but there's no doubt it's partly a consequence of the aggressive secularization of Western culture. A secularist worldview has three related components that will probably seem familiar to you.[2]

First is the assumption that the individual is the ultimate authority over his own existence, including his decisions and behavior. This is **individualism**. In this view, we're free to do what we want and define who we are. The Church's social teaching is in direct conflict with individualism. Of course, the Church is not against individual persons; she affirms the value of each person because we are each made in the image and likeness of God. However, she sees the darkness lurking behind secularist individualism because it makes many evils (not the least of which is abortion) sound rational.

Individualism often leads to the second component of secularism: **relativism**. Relativism is so dominant in Western society that we hardly notice it anymore. It assumes there are no objective moral standards that apply to everyone: I am free to define reality and truth for myself because these are mere constructs of culture. The right thing to do is anything that makes me feel good, no matter how much it hurts me or others, no matter how much it conflicts with reason and science. If moral standards are entirely culturally constructed and there is no objective right and wrong, justice requires that I alone define what is right for me, depending on my desires. If anybody opposes me, they are hateful or dumb. I've seen in my lifetime the slippery slope of relativism. Behaviors and values that were unthinkable in society only twenty years ago are now accepted as cool and desirable. As a result of the normalizing of relativism in education, the media, and the public square, we are witnessing a moral chaos that is destroying the dignity of humanity. From a Catholic worldview, there is an objective truth and a revealed moral law that act together as a compass point, helping us thrive as human beings. The moral law is not the enemy of human freedom, but the path to it.

Third, secularism assumes **scientific naturalism.** In this view, reality is limited to what can be measured and what we can experience with our five senses. Accordingly, faith, hope, and love are not real; truth, beauty, and goodness are not real.

There is nothing beyond this physical world, so there is no heaven, no God. I won't get into why this interpretation of reality is contradicted by science itself, but suffice it to say, scientific naturalism is taught with quasi-religious conviction in many of our schools, at every level. Catholics know, however, that there is no conflict between faith and reason. Pope St. John Paul II put it beautifully in *Fides et Ratio*: "Faith and reason are like two wings on which the human spirit rises to the contemplation of truth; and God has placed in the human heart a desire to know the truth — in a word, to know himself — so that, by knowing and loving God, men and women may also come to the fullness of truth about themselves."[3] God has placed in our hearts a desire to understand the world and how it works because our searching leads us to a greater understanding of God, ourselves, and our purpose in the world.

The crisis of faith in young people is undoubtedly fueled partly by these different components of secularism. Frankly, it's also fueled by concupiscence. Teenagers and young adults (and old adults!) sometimes make sinful choices and sacrifice common sense to have a little reckless fun on Friday nights.

In addition, some kids will do anything as long as their friends are doing it; they take their cues about what is desirable or good from their peers. These teens are peer-oriented. Since World War II, teenagers have become increasingly attached to peers while simultaneously detaching from the adults who are responsible for their well-being. Teenagers were never meant to raise other teenagers. Our teens' peers can't keep them spiritually, emotionally, or even physically safe, and our teens know it. The consequences of peer orientation are increasing alarm (anxiety, depression, self-harm) and delayed maturation. I'll unpack the problem of peer orientation and how parents can handle it in the next chapter.

Parents Are the Answer

Those obstacles are daunting, but where there are faithful parents like you, there is hope. You are a sign of the Holy Spirit active in the world, bringing about God's will. While the decline of religiosity and spirituality in our youth is troubling, and while secularism presents us with difficult obstacles in evangelizing our children, parents are the answer to these obstacles.

You are the answer. Not your parish's new teen evangelization program (which is probably fantastic) or youth minister (also probably fantastic). As somebody who has been involved in catechesis for many years, I am grateful for the abundant and attractive resources available for delivering faith formation to our youth. The folks who put these programs together think about what appeals to teens and the questions they ask. Many of these programs are lifesavers for parish leaders crafting youth ministry, often with minimal volunteer support. But any program is rendered nearly inert without the power of family catechesis and the lead of loving parents.

In fact, I have more study results for you. I think you'll be encouraged. In the largest-scale study ever done on religion and family across generations, analysts found that the single factor most likely to predict the successful transmission of faith from one generation to the next was ... warm, affirming parent-child relationships.[4] There's more good news for faithful parents. Several studies reveal a strong correlation between the serious faith practice of parents and the internalizing of faith in their adolescent and young adult children. We also find that teenagers who serve and lead at church are more likely to continue practicing their faith in early adulthood.[5]

What can we take away from this? While it's true that teen faith drift is common, it's not inevitable. These factors (parental warmth, parental modeling of faith, and teen service), which we'll explore in later chapters, show that there is much parents can do to cooperate with God as he draws our children toward a mature sacramental and spiritual life as Christians. The Son of God did not die on the cross to let a bunch of cranky secularists have the last word. Grace is real. The power of the sacraments is real. The intercession of the saints is real. The unceasing work of our Lord in the minds and hearts of his beloved children is real. We may feel like little workers in this great vineyard, but our work as parents is valuable and irreplaceable.

Jesus Isn't a Pair of Pants (and Other Reasons I Want My Kids to Be Catholic)

Should I really care that my teenager is Catholic? Shouldn't I let him make his own decisions about something as important as religious commitment? We have such questions because we live in a society that views religious practice as one choice among many other equally valid choices for how we spend our time. Church is a kind of therapy session, self-improvement program, or social club, so if my kid isn't getting anything out of it or making enough friends, we figure we should let him do something different. Maybe he could join a soccer team, learn to play the fiddle, or whittle small wooden animals while we're at Mass receiving the Body and Blood of our Lord.

Let's resist these ideas and shepherd our teenagers a little longer. We've planted the seeds of our children's faith. Now, as they navigate their teen years, it's time to nourish and nurture that faith, not allow it to wither.

Reasons to Love the Catholic Church

1. The Church provides a road map to human fulfillment.
2. Jesus founded the Church.
3. The Church is beautiful.
4. The Church is true.

As a revert to the Church, let me share with you why I want

to instill in my kids a love for the one, holy, catholic, and apostolic Church. First, I care that my kids are Catholic because the Church provides a roadmap to human fulfillment. All humans possess a natural interior inclination to the transcendent, and I would be hurting my children by pretending this inclination doesn't exist. I would be surrendering them to a lie that broke my own heart and continues to break the hearts of many people I know. The truth is that loss of faith is correlated to a loss of well-being. The deep dissatisfaction that is common in Western society is primarily rooted in a sense that life has no meaning, and we have no purpose because we have no destination. People try to fill their God-shaped emptiness with counterfeits like eating, promiscuity, wealth, and accolades. It never works.

Living in a me-sized box blinds us to reality and our innate dignity. Our Catholic Faith frees us from our boxes and provides direction in our search for meaning. Think of the virtues, the works of mercy, the Beatitudes, the lives of the saints, which give us some sense of how to be a decent human being and what real love looks like. Our Faith provides many answers to the most critical questions we will ever ask: What's the meaning of life, why are we here, what is really valuable, and what is our ultimate destination? The Church has spent 2000 years thinking about these questions, and she's come up with some good answers. The search alone brings purpose and clarity to our lives, and thankfully we don't have to figure out everything ourselves.

The teen years are no time to let our child disengage from the Faith so he can figure out life on his own. He needs the structure, guidance, and tools of the Church to help him figure all that out. In fact, the teen years are the perfect time to begin leading teenagers in exploring their spiritual lives more seriously. They're asking themselves questions about how to act, who to become, and the nature of true friendship. They need the Faith now more than ever. We want to help our teens build their lives on a foundation of real freedom and real love, and they will find that foundation only in Holy Mother Church.

Second, I care that my kids are Catholic because Jesus founded the Catholic Church. Now, some folks say Christ didn't found any church, and that as long as you're a nice person and believe in Jesus and his message, then that's all Jesus wants. No need to belong to any particular group of his followers. But the earliest Christians would disagree: They believed that Jesus established an authoritative Church, and they were concerned with protecting it.[6] If you ever get a chance, read the early Church Fathers, many of whom wrote before the New Testament was penned; your faith will be emboldened and enlightened. The early Church had a hierarchical structure, with a pope (the Bishop of Rome), bishops, priests, and deacons; it celebrated and prayed to saints. Though the ceremonial rubrics changed over time, early Masses had many rituals that would be familiar to us: readings, a homily, and the consecration.[7] One thing did not change, and it was the clincher that led to my return to the Church: The early Christians believed in the Real Presence of Jesus in the Eucharist. They didn't believe the bread was a symbol of Jesus; they believed the Body and Blood of the Lord was truly present in the Host.[8]

Third, I care that my kids are Catholic because the Faith is beautiful. The other Abrahamic religions (Judaism and Islam) de-emphasize artistic expressions of divine realities. Early Protestant Christians generally preferred plain worship settings because of their suspicion of ornament, which they interpreted as decadent frippery that could lead believers astray rather than a reminder of God's beauty and a fitting way to honor him. Some early Protestant denominations prohibited (and some modern ones prohibit) music of any kind in their worship, including sacred music. Early Protestant reformers destroyed precious Catholic art, baptismal fonts, stained glass, and altarpieces, disrupting the way of life of poor, illiterate parishioners who used the beauty of their parishes as a kind of worship aid.[9] The Catholic Church, on the other hand, has long appreciated the fine arts, recognizing that God reveals himself not only in truth and moral goodness but also in beauty. For centuries, the Church has inspired and evangelized the world through the spiritual truths communicated in our art, cathedrals, and sacred music. Beauty is a powerful form of catechesis, awakening us to the transcendent, shaping our hearts and minds. We celebrate and embrace beauty, because we know that the way of beauty is the way to Christ. I could never in my lifetime plumb the depths of the beauty produced by and for the Church.

Finally, I care that my kids are Catholic because the Faith is true. *It is true*. Catholic convert Brandon Vogt puts it like this: "God is real; Jesus is God; Jesus founded the Catholic Church. If all three of these statements are true, then Catholicism is true."[10] We can prove the existence of God through philosophical reason and from evidence in the universe. We can prove from historical evidence and eyewitness testimony that Jesus of Nazareth was real, that he had a group of devoted followers, and that he suffered a horrible death by crucifixion. Many eyewitnesses reported the miracles performed by Jesus; even non-Christian writers wrote about Jesus doing "marvelous" things (miracles). Jesus' many disciples attested to his resurrection, and they refused to renounce their beliefs even when facing death. I explained above why it's reasonable to claim that Jesus Christ founded the Church. Volumes have been written teasing out these arguments for the truth of our Faith; I find them more compelling than arguments to the contrary. Even if some members of the Church are flawed, even while some other world religions and non-Catholic Christian denominations possess some rays of truth, the Catholic Church possesses the fullness of Truth. And I want to be there — every day. So many things in my life are unsure, but I am blessed and privileged to call the true Church my home.

So, yes, I want my kids to be Catholic, and my primary mission as a disciple parent is to pass on the true Faith to my children. I do give my kids choices in some things. They can pick which pants they wear; they can pick whether they have fudge or caramel on their ice cream; I even let my older daughter pick her hair color. These are morally neutral choices. But Jesus Christ is not a pair of pants. Rejecting him is not a morally neutral choice. Choosing to pursue a false religion will ultimately lead my child to partial truth or even chaos. Choosing to live detached from faith will lead my child to the imprisonment of secularism, a false view of reality and human nature, and maybe even hell.

Until they're adults, we should continue the holy work of evangelizing our children. Of course, when they become adults, they may well make choices we disagree with. They may even do the wrong thing, knowing full well they are harming themselves or others. They may reject the Faith for ill-founded reasons and without interest in pursuing the truth. If that happens, our role will be to pray and surrender them to God. But, moms and dads, for now, while our kids are still under our daily care, we're responsible for them. We're not being pushy or controlling by wanting to transmit the Faith to our teenagers; we're being prudent, wise, and even courageous parents who love our children enough to do something hard.

Give Your Teen a Faith L.I.F.T.

When we shepherd teenagers, we no longer carry them like newborn lambs. We still lead, guide, and protect them, as we did when they were young, but we also allow them to explore in the field of life as they grow in wisdom and virtue. We provide opportunities for our teens to explore their faith and unique gifts, allow them to take reasonable risks, and encourage them to take on increasing responsibility. We even let them fail, then show them how to recover. When we shepherd our teens this way, we don't carry them like lambs, but we do cooperate with God by giving them a "L.I.F.T." toward more mature faith and a life of discipleship. L.I.F.T. stands for lead, inspire, free, and transform; the rest of the book is structured upon this acronym. As we *lead* our teens with love, through the grace of God, we will discover that moments arise naturally in everyday family life for *inspiring* them in the Faith. From this foundation, God will use us to *free* our teens from sin and *transform* them as they are drawn to something bigger than themselves. God works through us to shepherd these teens along as they become increasingly capable of growing in integrity and spiritual wisdom.

Where We're Headed

While our role in our teen's life is no less critical than when they were little, it does shift during adolescence. This book clarifies how our role changes and why that change is an opportunity, not a crisis. You'll learn to navigate through rough terrain as you shepherd and L.I.F.T. your teen on his or her spiritual journey.

Lead

- In chapter one, we'll look at how we transition from being the director to more of a mentor, guide, and facilitator in our teen's life. I explain the basic stages of faith development, particularly as they relate to our teens, and the critical role parents play in healthy faith development.

- In chapter two, we'll see how our teen's attachment to us now helps him become attached to God in adulthood. You'll discover why all teens need and desire a safe harbor to return to when the waters of life become too choppy. Many parents are surprised to learn that the safest harbor for an adolescent is not in peers but in his parents and other trusted adults.

Inspire

- Chapter three encourages you to introduce the idea of mission to your teen as early as possible. I'll explain why teens are more likely to internalize their faith when parents help them identify their spiritual gifts and engage them in practicing the works of mercy.
- Chapter four unpacks the idea of the "attachment village." In the teen years, we can facilitate our teen's connection to safe adults who can help him explore his interests, deepen his faith, and consider vocations. I'll explain "youth group flipped" and the power of multi-family and intergenerational catechesis. I'll also encourage you to use the youth program already in place in your parish to stoke the flames of your teen's love for God.

Free

- In chapter five, we'll see how the Church's tools of discernment can help our teens sort through tough choices about who they want to become, what they want to do with their lives, and how to recognize true friendship.
- Many parents deal with conflict with their teens, even when they had a close relationship when their teens were younger. Sometimes the change seems to happen overnight, and parents panic. In chapter six, I'll address common sources of conflict between teens and their parents, including sexuality, technology, and resistance to faith. I'll provide some

insights about how you can reduce conflict and how to protect your relationship with your teen when you do have conflict.

Transform

- In chapter seven, I'll explain why some teens flunk adolescence because they resist the necessary rites of passage from adolescence to adulthood. We'll see how parents can recapture or institute beautiful rituals that celebrate a teen's emerging maturity.
- Finally, in chapter eight, I turn my attention to you, mom or dad. Sometimes we suffer as parents because we are holding on to something that no longer works, we don't trust God to do his work, or we are weighed down by fear. Part of being a disciple parent is knowing what is and is not our job in transmitting faith to our kids.

Grab your shepherd's staff, because we have some teenagers to lead! Let's do this!

Lead

Lead

1

Gaining Insight into Your Teen's Faith Journey

I will set shepherds over them who will care for them, and they shall fear no more, nor be dismayed, neither shall any be missing, says the LORD.

— JEREMIAH 23:4

The Big Picture

- Understanding the stages of faith development in children and teens
- How a child's earliest relationships prepare him for

> a relationship with God
> - Peer orientation: the Trojan horse parents don't recognize

When our children are little, we direct their faith lives, and they pretty much believe what we tell them — more or less. But as they enter the teen years, our role changes because their understanding of the world changes. They witness the failures of adult Christians; they notice conflicting opinions between decent Catholics; they observe friends making choices that seem to make these friends popular and happy. They see these things, and they begin to question and doubt. The thing is, these experiences of uneasiness and instability are part of the process of coming to mature faith, but many kids never get past them. Sometimes they never receive good answers to their questions, so their reasonable doubt turns to apathy, cynicism, or hostility. Sometimes they are waylaid on their spiritual path by wolves dressed as professors. Sometimes we contribute to the problem by making them feel guilty for having doubts or questions, so they stop asking questions to make us happy.

We also contribute to the problem when we back away from leading our teen in his faith journey. While our role as our child's faith leader changes in the teen years, it does not end. Our teens must face the rough terrain of adolescence; it is a necessary rite of passage to adulthood. Our children need us to be confident and strong leaders, committed to getting them safely through the rocky pastures and pitfalls of childhood and adolescence. With our encouragement and guidance, they can arrive on the other side of the terrain with an emboldened faith that creates an anchor in their lives. Let's look at how teen faith development unfolds and the role parents play in this process.

Stages of Faith Development

Nourishing the faith of teens requires different "fertilizer" than the faith of a young child. A teen's faith appetite and nutritional needs change, just as their biological appetite and nutritional needs change. Adolescent faith development is a distinct stage on the journey toward mature discipleship. Theorists have several ways of conceptualizing the stages of faith development. Here, I'm drawing mostly on John Westerhoff's four-stage "styles" of faith.[1] As catechist Frank Mercadante explains Westerhoff's concept: "Faith develops by adding to (not replacing) already acquired faith styles and experiences. We do not outgrow previous faith styles, but continue to build upon the faith experiences of past stages throughout our lives."[2] So, Westerhoff sees faith as developing not necessarily in sequential stages that we outgrow and leave behind, but in patterns that we incorporate and integrate as we mature spiritually. Additionally, like all aspects of human development, these are *potential* stages of growth, but not *inevitable* stages. Just as emotional development can be arrested, faith development can remain stagnant at an early stage for many decades.[3]

Imitative faith (little kids)

Emotionally healthy preschoolers and school-aged children tend to imitate the faith of their parents, just as they imitate how their parents talk and dress. They want to be like their parents, so they believe what their parents believe, and they love what their parents love, for the most part (my kids drew the line at green vegetables when they were little!). This imitative behavior is not only completely healthy, but it's one aspect of a crucial stage of human development, as I will explain in the next chapter. Faith at this stage is less intellectual and more sensorial and emotional.

Children benefit from the beautiful sights, sounds, and smells of our Faith, even if they don't understand what they signify; they delight in the stories and rituals of our Faith, even if they don't understand their doctrinal foundations. When a child experiences his parent's consistent love, particularly during faith experiences, later he will believe more easily that God loves him. As I explain below, a child's first experiences in his relationship with his parents create a lens through which the child interprets later relationships, including his relationship with God.

Affiliative faith (tweens and young teens)

If young children have their imitative faith needs met, they may enter the affiliative faith stage in the tween and teen years. Still somewhat imitative in nature, at this stage, the young believer yearns to belong to a community with a strong sense of identity and "to make a contribution to its life."[4] They want to belong, and they want to be significant to the faith community. As I'll explain in the next chapter, this yearning for belonging and significance is an important aspect of emotional development. There, I'll offer some practical tips for meeting these needs, but here I want to underscore that, without guidance and mentoring, teens will go anywhere they can feel this sense of belonging and significance. It's essential that we match our teens to adults at our parishes and help them find avenues for contributing their gifts in our parishes. I'll talk more about this matchmaking in chapter four.

Kids at this stage tend to accept what their parents and faith formation teachers tell them about God, though they may ask simple questions from a place of good-natured curiosity. While intellectual formation is important, we can't forget about the heart. The young believer at the affiliative stage possesses affection for the Faith, so this is a great time to fan the flames of that natural affection. In *Discipleship Parenting*, I encourage parents to evangelize their children through the power of beauty. The beauty of our Faith inspires awe and wonder about the Author of it. Children and teenagers are responsive to beauty because their aesthetic awareness blossoms far earlier than their logical and moral reasoning do. So, surround your children with the beauty found in Catholicism's great treasury of architecture, art, and music.

Without nurturance and support, the teenager will remain at the affiliative faith stage for many years, possibly for the rest of his life. Or he may become frustrated with the faith of his childhood and search elsewhere to get his needs met. Many adult Catholics have never grown beyond the affiliative faith stage.

Searching faith (older teens; young adults)
Toward later adolescence, we may see flashes of maturity in our teen's faith life that reveal a searching style of faith. The teen may begin taking the initiative in his faith journey, asking for permission to sign up for retreats, Eucharistic adoration, or other events at his parish. Searching faith "embodies the need to commit our lives to persons and causes," but teens often jump from one cause and commitment to the next as they experiment and explore.[5] They can seem erratic and even flaky, which creates occasional conflict with parents.

Also alarming for many parents is the fact that searching and doubting often go hand-in-hand. Note, not all teens experience doubts, but yours might. As their faith matures, teens begin moving from a strictly community-based faith to a more personal faith in which they seek answers to their honest questions about God's existence and the Church's teachings. Your teen may question specific teachings, not necessarily out of anger or cynicism, but because he is intellectually capable of comparing what he's been taught as a child to what he is learning in other settings, like school, peer groups, and social media. He may become curious about other faith traditions or even about the claims of atheists.

The Church distinguishes between "voluntary doubt," in which a person refuses to believe revealed truth, and "involuntary doubt," in which a person experiences "hesitation in believing, difficulty in overcoming objections connected with the faith, or also anxiety aroused by its obscurity" (*Catechism of the Catholic Church* 2088). Healthy teens can have this hesitation of belief, where they begin to lose confidence in what they know about God. This is very different from an unhealthy, hostile, sneering rejection of God. While we should never permit our teenagers' curiosity to lead to apostasy, we should be open to discussing the truth claims of these other groups.

Share with your teen your own curiosity and questions about the Church's teachings, and model how you deal with them: You read and pray; you ask questions; you remain faithful through your doubts. Welcome your teen's questions and invite him to look for answers with you. Share how God delights in our questions; he gave us these inquiring minds! In this way, you're sending your teen the message that you aren't afraid of his questions, and neither is God. In chapter two I offer tips for "No Topic Off the Table" nights, which are special times you set aside for your teen to explore his questions about God, the Church, and the Church's teachings. If you feel you're in over your head, ask for help from a youth minister or priest at your parish.

Many teenagers, at some point, doubt the existence of God. I did not appreciate this when my oldest was a teenager, because at the time he never told me that he was having doubts. However, when he was about twenty, I was telling him about Westerhoff's model and the doubting that often accompanies the searching faith stage. He told me that he began to doubt God's existence in ninth grade, but our parish youth minister answered all his questions and welcomed him to ask more. He said his faith grew stronger because he was allowed to be honest about his doubts, and he had a mentor willing to work through these doubts with him. I now tell all my kids when they're about ten that they may doubt God's existence at some point in the next few years, and that if that happens, it's just a sign that they are growing up spiritually, and I'll do my best to answer their questions.

While uncomfortable for parents, this is a necessary stage of spiritual development. The teen can't skip over it to the next stage of faith. Depending on how he and the adults around him handle this stage, he will come out of it with either a more resilient faith or a stagnant, fading faith. Without working through the crisis of this stage, he may revert to an affiliative faith or reject faith altogether. Or he may become a Sunday Catholic who shows up to Mass out of a sense of obligation and not because he is convinced by truth, committed to the Church, or changed by Christ. (Attending Mass out of a sense of obligation is not a bad thing; it gets us all through periods of dryness. However, ideally, we continue growing in our relationship with God, our understanding of the gifts of the Church, and our gratitude for the graces of the sacraments.)

A word of caution: We should never allow our teens to explore their doubts and questions in isolation. I'm not talking about the teen taking walks alone to think or spending time alone in thought and prayer; this sort of solitude is healthy, as I'll explain in the next chapter. We should see our teen spending time in solitude balanced by conversations with trusted spiritual guides. If the teen thinks he can go it alone when he has doubts about God or the Church, this is not a sign of blossoming faith, but fear, mistrust, or even pride. Christ left a Church for us because he knew we couldn't survive the journey of faith alone. A person genuinely moving through the searching faith stage doesn't leave behind his faith community to begin his search; he brings his appreciation for and reliance on his faith community into this new stage that will lead ultimately to a more personal connection to Christ. In chapter six on managing challenges with your teen, I will share some tips on what to do if your teen refuses to allow you or other adults to lead him as he works through his faith struggles.

Owned faith (early adulthood or later)

Giving our teen permission to have a searching faith — with all its chaos and uncertainty — will prepare him for owned faith. At this stage, the Christian plants his stake in the Faith and calls it his own. He is a true disciple, a follower of Christ who wants to see, think, and love like Christ. He still faces doubts and setbacks, but his faith is growing, his relationship with God deepening, and his commitment to the Church unwavering. While he values his Catholic roots and the foundation his family provided for him, he isn't Catholic only because his family is Catholic. He has made a conscious choice to be Catholic.

Think of it like this:

- Imitative faith repeats, "This is what we do."
- Affiliative faith says, "If you believe it, I believe it."
- Searching faith asks, "Is this what I really believe?"
- Owned faith declares, "This is what I believe! This is who I am!"

Owned faith becomes central to one's identity and increasingly informs one's choices and perceptions. In short, we are transformed by owned faith. I will unpack this stage a bit more toward the end of the book when I talk about where we want our kids to be headed in their faith lives as they enter adulthood. Because our teens pay attention to what matters to us, consider where you are on your faith journey. Why are you Catholic? Did you experience a point in your faith journey when you crossed a threshold and realized you wanted to choose the Faith for yourself? Do you feel chosen and cherished as a child of God? If not, where are you stuck? Wherever you are on this journey, you can grow in faith alongside your teen.

To recap: If a child grows up in a warm, nurturing home with parents who live their faith positively, then the child will naturally transition from the imitative faith stage to the affiliative faith stage in the early teen years. Then, if the teen is surrounded by encouraging adults who invite him into community, continue drawing him close even when he stumbles, accompany him as he discovers his unique gifts and talents, then he will transition naturally into the searching faith stage. Many teenagers in our parishes who take an interest in parish programs are on the bridge between affiliative faith and searching faith. They may hang around on the bridge longer than necessary because they're fearful of facing their doubts, or they're fearful they'll lose the acceptance of their families or faith communities if they ask too many questions. If the older teen is fortunate to have patient adult companions who will help him as he wrestles with the uneasiness of searching faith, he has a better chance of making it over the bridge and onto a lifetime path of discipleship.

Your Finest Shepherd's Tool

Some teens struggle at the searching faith stage because they suffer from emotional wounds that leave them unable to trust others, including God. Some people want to know Christ and grow spiritually, but they feel stuck. They know things — they can understand the Faith intellectually, but they struggle to grow spiritually because they never experience God's presence and peace. God remains "the guy over there" who never invites them into the circle; they are left outside and isolated.

I felt this way for many years. I was an intellectual convert; I learned as much as I could about the history and teachings of the Church. I knew I had found the Church founded by Jesus Christ, and I was an enthusiastic revert. But I felt cut off from God. I assented to the statement that God loved me, but on a real heart level, I wasn't sure he was much interested in me. I guess I figured he was too busy to pay attention to me. Spiritual directors asked me to visualize myself in scenes from the Gospels, so that I could better encounter Jesus or see myself as one of his disciples. Inevitably in those meditations, I was lost in the crowd. I was invisible to Christ. I would be there, watching Jesus, but he was too busy with other people to notice me. I knew God was capable of helping me, but it felt like he chose to attend to others instead. I told many people closest to me that I felt like a spiritual orphan. Perhaps you can identify with my experience.

I don't want to oversimplify a complex spiritual struggle. There are many reasons earnest seekers experience periods of dryness or desolation in their spiritual lives. For example, spiritual flatness can occur when we take a wrong turn, and God wants us to pay attention — the flatness is a grace helping us get back on track. Yet, emotional wounds are certainly another reason some of us struggle to find peace and intimacy in our relationship with God, who is truly active in our lives, always inviting us to come closer to him through the sacraments and in prayer.

Dr. Tim Clinton uses the term "soul wounds" to describe attachment injuries that occur early in our lives and impact all our relationships later, including our relationship with God:

> Attachment injuries occur when, in times of stress, we expect a loved one to be there for us, and for whatever reason, he or she is not. ... Most simply, an early attachment injury results when someone we love, somebody who we think should love us, like a parent, fails to provide our fundamental safety and security needs. ... And such injuries can ignite life's core pains: anger, anxiety, fear, grief, and suffering of various kinds.[6]

Attachment is a word people tend to associate with parenting infants, but attachment is simply the science of relationships — all relationships, not just infant-caregiver relationships. The essence of attachment is the drive within all of us to pursue and preserve proximity to the people we depend on to meet our needs. These people are our attachment figures. While our parents are our first attachment figures, we will continue to have attachment figures for our entire lives. These are the people we rely on for a sense of safety and "home."

We are wired with this drive at birth, and it animates our reactions and choices every day. Quite simply, contact and connection to our attachment figures is our preeminent need, and separation from our attachment figures is our preeminent threat.[7] When we experience a threat of separation — even a perceived threat — from our attachment figure, our brains move us to restore proximity, often through pursuit of the attachment figure or an adaptation of our behavior to keep the attachment figure close.

A Caveat: Social Science, the Church, and Human Flourishing

Before we dive deeper into the science of attachment, I want to say a word about the current state of the social sciences. I'm grateful for the social sciences. In particular, grasping the significance of human attachment helped me immensely in my mothering. The social sciences ask questions about human flourishing, so we value the insights and information gleaned there. I recognize, however, that we must be prudent when reading parenting advice rooted in secular psychological theories. The hard sciences (physics, chemistry, biology) differ from the social sciences in how they handle new findings. In the former, new findings that have been replicated are automatically synthesized, but in the social sciences, this synthesis is avoided and even suppressed, particularly in controversial areas.[8] To put it bluntly, social scientists are often more

concerned with ideology than science. This problem is most pro-
nounced in studies of marriage and family, sexuality, and religious
practice. While I think it's an overreaction to dismiss everything
in the social scientific literature with a broad sweep, we must be
mindful that all scientists (including those in the hard sciences)
begin with a particular understanding of the human person that
can shape and distort their observations and interpretations of
data, and some social scientists come to their work with specific
outcomes in mind.

The social sciences can help us understand human flourishing, but we should question anything that conflicts with the
Church's teachings on the dignity and nature of the human person. We should be skeptical of any claims that flourishing results
from unfettered sexual freedom or the freedom to redefine our
own natures. And flourishing is always thwarted when we use our
freedom to use others to satisfy our own needs or to engage in
morally disordered relationships or activities. True flourishing
means we're growing toward greater perfection and holiness. We
flourish as we become more virtuous and, therefore, increasingly
capable of using our freedom to make wise choices that suit our
particular state in life. Drawing on the work of many exemplary
Christian writers and practitioners, I endeavor here to integrate
the Catholic understanding of the person with what I find insightful in psychological sciences; our Faith can sharpen what is good
in the social sciences and correct what is wrong or unreliable.

Attachment Is about More than Cuddling

Human beings have one drive to attach to each other but different
"modes" of attaching.[9] Infants and babies have an intense need for
physical closeness because they attach through physical touch and
proximity — they want to be held by and near their mommies and
daddies. Older kids, teens, and adults also need physical closeness,
but the kind of proximity they seek is more than physical. As hu-

mans mature, they become capable of attaching to others through other more sophisticated forms of "proximity": a sense of sameness, belonging, significance, emotional intimacy, and psychological intimacy. We'll dive deeper into these other forms of closeness in the next chapter, but I introduce them here to emphasize the purpose and power of attachment. These ways of connecting with our attachment figures help us come to rest emotionally so that we can grow, explore, and play. Our attachments give us a feeling of rootedness and safety so that we can enjoy life. We are more creative, imaginative, and vital because of the people in our lives who make us feel "at home."

Our children's attachment to us also gives us the power to keep them safe and lead them to maturity. A critical insight: Children will only follow people they are attached to. For this reason, attachment is our finest shepherd's tool as we lead our teenagers through the pitfalls and dangers of the modern world. If our teens experience us as the answer to their deepest needs, they will follow our lead as we shepherd them through the stages of their emotional and intellectual development. If they are attached to us, they can lean on us when life feels like too much; from this secure base, they can go off to explore, knowing we will be there if they need us. This is also true for their faith development: Attachment gives us the power to shepherd our teenagers toward more mature faith. If they are attached to us, they can lean on us and trust us through the anxieties of the searching faith stage.

The Dance of Attachment: Dependence and Caretaking

Dr. Gordon Neufeld describes the dynamic of attachment as a dance between one person in the dependent mode and another person in the caretaking mode. Metaphorically (or literally with little children and their parents), one person reaches up in a stance of need while the other person reaches down to be the answer to the need. This dance occurs in every single attachment relationship, including between adult friends and married couples. In adult relationships, this dance is reciprocal. Sometimes one person reaches up to be cared for, which moves the other person to reach down to care for them. So maybe one evening, we notice our spouse sighing and tossing his shoes into the closet with an irritated flick. We know he's had a bad day. We're moved to be the answer to what our spouse needs at this point. We metaphorically lean down to comfort and encourage. But the next day, we might have a cold, so our spouse gets the kids ready for school and brings us a cup of tea. In healthy adult relationships, the two people alternate between dependence and caretaking.

In healthy adult-child relationships (including with teenagers), the dance of attachment is never reciprocal, at least when we're talking about emotional needs. Always, without exception, the parent should take the caretaking stance, and the child should remain in the dependent role. The parent is moved to be the answer to cues from the child that he needs help, support, or encouragement, and indeed the parent often moves in to provide that care, even before the child cues it. Children thrive in hierarchical relationships in which they can take for granted that their grown-ups will protect and care for them. Without secure attachments to their parents, children become preoccupied with seeking the parents — seeking comfort, assurance, compliments.

Think of the yearning for safe attachment as a cup that can be empty, full, or somewhere in between. When the dance of attachment works well, the parent keeps topping up the child's attachment cup so the child never feels empty. These intuitive parents anticipate their children's needs and build into the relationship more attachment-nurturing exchanges than the child needs to merely survive. For example, the parents don't give the children just enough attention to keep them from bothering them, or just enough snuggles to calm them down. Throughout the day, they have simple rituals and habits that top up that attachment cup. As I'll explain further in the next chapter, it is in this state of attachment satiation that our children are free to grow up.

Children should never feel responsible for meeting a parent's emotional needs, but they should certainly express love, concern, and respect for their parents, and older children can certainly care for younger siblings who need help. And, of course, our children can step in to contribute to the upkeep of our homes, as appropriate for their developmental age. We want our domestic churches to foster self-giving love, but we don't want our children to feel it's their responsibility to save us or fix us.

The Dance of Attachment with Teens

One of the developmental tasks of the teen years is learning to stand on your own two feet and become competent to make your way in the world. This process of maturing occurs naturally in the context of safe attachment relationships.[10] The dance of attachment must continue through the teen years. Teens intuitively know that they need the care and guidance of others to become fully functioning adults, but they face a crisis of attachment. Even though we'll always be their parents, our teens experience growing up as a kind of separation. If separation is our greatest human fear, our teens are on high alert. They anticipate one of the defining separations of human development: leaving the safety of home to enter the wilderness of life. Teens know the comforts and simplicity of childhood are coming to an end, and the uncertainty of adulthood looms large.

On top of this, teens experience an attachment "void" as they prepare to separate from home. This is a developmental space or gap in their identities that God means them to fill with a refined vision of themselves and their relationships. Their idealized views of their parents and teachers fade. They realize we don't know everything, and sometimes we do things we warn them not to do, and they feel a void. They once felt deeply known by their parents; they saw themselves through their parents' eyes. Now, as their minds and bodies mature, they hardly know who they are. They feel like a stranger to themselves, and they feel a void. The loneliness and sadness many teens feel are a natural effect of this developmental crisis. These are emotions that accompany a necessary loss that they must confront, mourn, and survive, and it is up to us to help them through it. Eventually, they should come to a place where they recognize God as the only flawless, faultless comforter; they should find forgiveness and patience for the flaws and faults in their parents and other people they care about. They eventually discover that only God knows them perfectly, but their parents know them pretty well, and when we miss the mark and misinterpret them, they can still trust us with their hearts.

While he does not write or teach from any particular religious perspective, Dr. Neufeld emphasizes how vital religious practices have been throughout history in helping youth transition to adulthood and how adults remain responsible for connecting youth to these practices.[11] Our faith practices and traditions, particularly those with long cultural roots, provide a structure for young people as they wrestle through the attachment void. So, we can emphasize faith traditions in our homes and keep our teens connected to the communities and rituals that can sustain them. Pope John Paul II understood the dangers of leaving teenagers to face the crises of adolescence alone. He spoke of adolescence as a time of "deeper questioning, of anguished even frustrating searching, of a certain mistrust of others and dangerous introspection"; he encouraged adults to help teenagers through this angst by pointing them toward "Jesus Christ as a Friend, Guide and Model" and the answer to life's fundamental questions.[12] Without adults guiding them, teens can fall prey to "dangerous introspection" — often obsessions with superficial pleasures or even darkness. Many teens try to fill the void with a false identity picked up from peers or YouTube influencers. They don't want to do the work of adolescence. Ideally, the void is like a window to the soul; when our teen looks through the window, he will see the seat of his being and a reflection of himself in his Creator.

While we can and must accompany them, ultimately, our teens must choose to face critical questions about themselves and their purpose in the world. Who am I? What do I value? What kind of person am I called to become? Answers to these questions must eventually fill the attachment void. In reality, a teen can flunk the tests of adolescence, and many do. They resist their developmental and transcendent destiny because they refuse to face the losses that come with growing up. Your teen needs you to help her survive the crisis. She needs you to help her fill the void not with technology or superficial relationships but with her growing sense of self and her identity as a child of God.

Yes, Your Teen Really Does Need You

You may doubt that your teenager needs — let alone *wants* — to be attached to you. Perhaps you sense her pulling away from you, shrinking inside her own world in some ways. You're probably right. She may be facing that attachment void and feeling many mixed emotions. Sometimes the emotions burst out in your face. Teens also experience an explosion of awareness that makes them a little self-absorbed. Small children think concretely; they tend to live life from one experience to the next without self-reflection. For the first time in their lives, teenagers become introspective as they develop an adult-type reflective consciousness.[13] They can consider their own feelings, thoughts, and ideas. They also become acutely aware of other people's awareness of them, which explains their tendency to be self-conscious and a bit over-sensitive to others' opinions about them. They assume everybody is far more interested in what they look like, think, and do than is probably the case. They assume everybody is as obsessed with them as they are with themselves! So, your once sweet little girl who would curl up in your lap with her favorite book now curls up in bed and groans when you mention family bowling night. This is not an indication that your teen isn't attached to you, or that you don't need to continue inviting the attachment. It's simply an indication that you are living with a teenager.

It's awkward sometimes and can cause friction, but don't walk away from the dance. Continue inviting. Your teen is wired for it; she wants the invitation. I will touch more on ways you can engage your teen's attachment instincts in the next chapter.

God Attachment and Our Search for Meaning

The attachment void is the beginning of a teen's search for meaning, which will continue for the rest of her life. It's the way God made us: We need to search for meaning in our lives, and we'll continue looking for it until we find it. We don't just need meaning. We find meaning in searching for meaning! We are a restless bunch — wondering, wandering, questioning, questing. Our searching hearts are like a homing system, drawing us toward our true home, where we can find ultimate meaning and happiness with God.

Attachment is intimately connected to this search for meaning. Safe attachments free us to experience awe, recognize beauty, and delight in the sublime. Safe attachments prepare us to encounter God and respond to him with trust. Not everyone immediately sees God as the answer to this yearning and search for meaning, but if we are free to search, we will eventually face the question of whether we want to be in relationship with God.

Our attachment figures help us understand what it means to feel secure in the care of another person so that, eventually, we can feel secure in God's care. Our earliest experiences in hierarchical attachment relationships create the lens through which we understand ourselves in relationship with God. This connection between our attachment status and our ability to attach to God has been explored in numerous fascinating, high-quality studies over many decades.[14]

Let's unpack what it looks like when a person has positive or negative early attachment experiences. Depending on these early experiences, a person develops assumptions and core beliefs about himself and others.[15] These assumptions and beliefs answer questions like:

Am I worthy of being loved? Am I capable of getting the love I need?

Are others trustworthy and capable of loving me? Are others available and willing to help me when I express my needs?

Secure Attachment

People who can answer these questions positively tend to have **secure attachment** in their relationships. Securely attached children tend to have parents who make them feel emotionally safe. The parents express delight in their children and tend to be emotionally warm and open. Their children feel welcomed, valued, and safe. Even when the child messes up, the parent continues to express love for the child; they set boundaries but avoid sending a message that bad behavior could end the relationship or damage the parent's love for the child. These parents tend to be comfortable with a wide range of emotions in their children, even if they need to help them express the emotions appropriately. As these children grow up, their basic assumptions about themselves and others allow their relationships to flourish. They feel worthy of being loved, and they believe others are capable and willing to love them. They can be angry with others without attacking; they have confidence that their thoughts and feelings matter.

These basic assumptions are at play in their relationship with God, too. Secure adults assume God is willing to love them, meet them in prayer, and respond to their needs. They assume God is interested in them. They are more likely to feel comfortable sharing their thoughts and feelings with God, even their disappointment and anger. God becomes their attachment figure: He is a safe haven in times of trouble and a secure base from which to explore the world with courage and confidence.

Insecure Attachment

When the dance of attachment goes awry, children become locked into behaviors to get their attachment needs met (intensified pursuit, whining, clinging). Sometimes these behaviors are temporary; the attachment dance begins again, and the child feels better and even builds resilience. However, when the dance goes awry chronically or permanently, deep attachment wounds occur. Children erect emotional defenses that tend to manifest in different ways, depending on how they feel in the relationship with their parents. These are called insecure attachment styles.

Children with **anxious attachment** don't experience predictable love and care from their parents. Sometimes the parent responds, sometimes not, so the child becomes preoccupied with pursuing the parent or checking for mood changes in the parent. They have a fragile sense of self. Often, they feel responsible for their parents' well-being. As they mature, they have a high opinion of others and a low opinion of themselves. Some anxious people focus excessively on their physical attractiveness. They tend to have intense emotions, yet they avoid disagreements and rarely express opinions that conflict with others' opinions. Because they don't speak their minds or share their feelings, they are incapable of real intimacy. They can feel resentful toward their loved ones, and sometimes the resentment surfaces with explosive anger that catches their loved ones off guard.

These patterns continue in their relationship with God. On the upside, many anxiously attached adults enter the owned faith stage. They can be wonderful parishioners and generous with sharing their gifts with others, yet they struggle to grow spiritually. They are interested in a relationship with God, but, deep down, they don't think God is interested in them. They avoid sharing their honest feelings with God for fear God will reject them. Significantly, at times of crisis, they don't turn to God for help. They believe they're on their own, just as they were always left on their own as children to self-soothe their pain and worries. They may feel resentment toward God for not being there for them. Author Joe Heschmeyer writes: "Our relationship with God is not that of servants or slaves, desperately trying to win the approval of the Master. Rather we are children already loved by the Father, already promised every good gift, up to and including the glories of heaven."[16] Here is the tragedy: Folks with anxious attachment never really feel like God's beloved children. They feel like the servant desperately trying to measure up; the outsider never invited to the banquet table.

A child who grows up with parents who are emotionally cold or intrusive may develop an **avoidant attachment** style in his relationships. Sometimes the parents extend love and acceptance only when the child achieves or wins, so the child grows up feeling his value is connected to external success. These children seem prematurely independent. As adults, they have an exiled sense of self, cut off from others. They have a high opinion of themselves and a low opinion of others. They resent neediness in others and avoid intimacy. In contrast to the anxiously attached person who seems very needy, the avoidant person acts like they don't need anybody. Some avoidant people have narcissistic personality traits, but under their veneer of superiority is a haunting sense that they are worthless. Avoidant adults are less likely to enter the owned faith stage at all because they don't see the point of a relationship with God. If they do remain practicing Catholics, they tend to do so for the social connections, status, or some other personal advantage. If they believe in God, they are more likely to lose their faith in a time of crisis. They are also more likely to act out in anger at God by flaunting sinful habits and ridiculing the Church's moral teaching.

When children grow up in an abusive home, they may develop a **disorganized attachment** style. They have the worst of both worlds: They assume they don't deserve love, and they don't believe the people around them who are responsible for their well-being can provide it. Abuse takes many forms: psychological, physical, emotional, and sexual. Intense marital conflict and addiction in a child's home also create abusive conditions. These children know they can't depend on their parents to take care of them, so they look for substitutes — peers, animals, objects. If a person with an anxious relationship style has a fragile self and the person with an avoidant style has an exiled self, the disorganized person has a shattered self. Their personalities seem fractured and unstable; they may struggle with addiction. Depending on their childhood experiences, they may experience God as unreliable and even cruel or wrathful.

These insecure attachment styles prevent people from flourishing. Their initial response to the emotional pain in their homes is natural — they erect defenses to protect themselves. All of us erect emotional defenses during stressful times, with people who seem unsafe to us, or when the attachment dance doesn't seem to be working with the people we count on most. We couldn't survive without these defenses. For most of us, the defenses eventually come down, our hearts soften, and the attachment dance begins again. But for these insecurely attached people, the defenses become part of their personalities, causing problems in their relationships, including with God.

What's Your Attachment Style?

If you are curious about your own attachment style, you can take attachment assessments with a psychologist or even find free online assessments.[17] However, these attachment styles are complicated. We can have a dominant style in most of our relationships, but in a few relationships, we can have other attachment styles. I tend to struggle with anxious attachment; I know it is my default attachment style, especially during times of stress. But in attachment assessments, I am avoidant in a few relationships, and I have a secure attachment status in my relationship with my husband. That leads to another important point: Your attachment status can change in adulthood. Healthy relationships can help you heal from early attachment wounds. I know that even with my anxious attachment style, I am now capable of healthy, mutually supportive friendships. Learning about the process of healthy attachment and working on my own anxious attachment helped not only my family relationships but also my relationship with God. I can now visualize myself in Gospel scenes with the disciples, and I feel personally held and cherished by God. So if you believe you may have attachment wounds, don't despair. God is not limited by our attachment wounds; he can heal them or at least lead us forward despite them.

I like to share attachment science with parents so they recognize the power of the parent-child relationship in shaping a child's future capacity for vulnerability, love, and trust in her adult relationships. Anybody interested in the faith lives of teens and young adults will benefit from understanding attachment. People with a secure attachment style will have an easier time navigating the searching faith stage and growing in the owned faith stage. While parents are a child's primary attachment figures when he's young, hopefully God eventually becomes the preeminent attachment figure in his life. Ultimately, we hope our teens come to see Jesus Christ and his Church as the answer to their search for a place to belong. We hope they come to see God as the answer to their yearning for a sense of meaning and direction. This is unlikely to happen until they enter the owned faith stage, though I have known many teens who are sincere seekers of deeper connection to God.

Until they are old enough and spiritually mature enough to plant a stake in the Faith — to own it — our children and teens need us and other safe adults to meet their attachment needs, because in meeting those needs, we are creating a model for them of what God is like. Is God dependable, loving, and interested in them? Or is God detached, angry, remote, and punishing? Through their encounters with us, especially during times of crisis, our children develop a gut-level perception of God. If our teens grow to trust God and experience him as caring, warm, and interested in their lives, they will be capable of being led through the uncertainties and anxieties of the searching faith stage. Even in the owned faith stage, they may wrestle with their trust in God, particularly during a crisis, but they become increasingly capable of turning to God with their needs. When our teens can lean on and trust God this way, they're securely attached to God. God becomes their safe haven during times of stress and a secure base as they explore potential vocations and their roles in the Church and society.

The Pesky Problem of Peer Orientation
The dance of attachment happens naturally between a parent and her child when the relationship is healthy. When the dance is working, the child feels secure and loved, while the parent feels confident and fulfilled. In generations past, parents didn't need to take parenting classes or read expert opinions to raise their

children. Most parents and their children engaged in the dance without thinking about it because culture and society facilitated what was natural in the relationships. The parents led; the children followed. Parents modeled how to work, how to love, even how to play; children emulated their example. In the last three or four generations, cultural shifts have disrupted the dance. In fact, it is more common now for the child and parent to be out of step — constantly negotiating, pushing, pulling. Parents and their children still love each other, but parents now have to be more intentional and countercultural in how they live with their children if they want to engage their children's attachment instincts.

The most vexing disruption to the attachment dance has been the rise of peer orientation. Dr. Neufeld has studied this phenomenon through a cross-disciplinary lens for many years, tracing the roots and consequences of peer orientation and how to prevent or reverse it.[18] Peer orientation happens when children emotionally orbit around each other rather than their parents and other adults responsible for them (teachers, religious leaders, coaches). Peer orientation is the Trojan horse of our generation: It's sitting right in front of us, it's dangerous, and most people don't realize it's a problem. In addition to being a mother of four, I teach literature, writing, and grammar to middle schoolers and high schoolers, and I've been involved in catechesis in different capacities for many years. I can tell you that peer orientation affects not only parenting but also schooling and catechesis — indeed, all settings in which adults are meant to lead children. Peer-oriented children are difficult to teach because they are hyper-focused on their peers' reactions and approval.[19] The peers are really doing the teaching, not the teacher.

A peer-oriented child looks to peers for cues about what to believe, how to behave, what to value, and even how to treat animals, other children, and adults. Throughout history, culture, language, and values have been transmitted vertically from one generation to the next. Now they are transmitted horizontally peer-to-peer. A peer-oriented child looks to her peers to be the answer to her attachment needs, so she will not follow the lead of the adults who are meant to keep her safe and help her grow up. A peer-oriented child turns to her peers for the answer to her deep attachment yearnings while at the same time turning away from her parents to be the answer to these needs. Because they know intuitively that a peer can never meet their needs, peer-oriented kids and teens are on heightened alert for signs of disapproval or rejection. They erect a manufactured self for their peers. This freezes maturation or at least renders it sluggish.

If the attachment dance has been working okay for centuries, then when and why did kids become peer-oriented? It began occurring rapidly in the mid-twentieth century when several cultural shifts intersected, creating a perfect storm.[20] The home shifted from agricultural production, where children and their older family members worked side by side, to industrial production where home and work became separated. Children spend more time with peers and less time with adult mentors than they did in previous generations. Another shift: Mothers moved into the workforce, leaving their children in the care of substitute attachment figures. This is not necessarily detrimental if the child is securely attached to the caregiver and the caregiver is warm and nurturing. However, teens are usually left home alone while both parents work. It seems that at this phase in their development, the substitute attachment figures become peers.[21] So, the detrimental effect on teen development from maternal employment seems to be rooted in the absence of adult care — the teens are left to fend for themselves. Without guidance and supervision, teens are more likely to engage in deviant and high-risk behaviors with their peers.

Harsh, controlling, and negligent parenting can contribute

to peer orientation, but peer orientation occurs even in loving homes because parents permit and even encourage it. Some parents probably assume peer orientation is entirely natural in teenagers. It is not natural. It might be the norm nowadays, but it's far from natural. I was surprised to learn that the concept of "teen culture" is a modern phenomenon; it did not exist prior to the twentieth century.[22] I was so skeptical about this claim when I first heard it in 2006 that I decided to ask an older relative about it. My great-aunt Irene was born in 1914, and she confirmed that there wasn't a distinct "teen culture" when she was young. She and her friends all wanted to be like their mothers. They were excited to wear dresses like their mothers' dresses. They were required to wear children's shoes until they were old enough for adult shoes. And what sort of adult shoes did she want? She could recall decades later the day she received her first pair of "lady shoes," like those her mother wore. Yes, she wanted to dress like her mom! In previous generations, youth looked up to their adults and wanted to be like the adults; now, teens want to be like one another.

It's bad enough that teens pick up their fashion tastes from each other (I expect that train has left the station and will never return), but it's far more concerning that they're so obsessed with one another's approval and acceptance. When a teen looks to peers to meet her emotional needs, she will be in a state of constant alarm because the peers are not equipped to meet her needs, and the threat of separation (rejection, judgment) is so intense. A peer-oriented teen remains developmentally stuck because she has nobody to guide her through the crises of adolescence. Let me clarify that it's okay and natural for teens to become attached to one another. Healthy teens have friends. However, peer *attachment* and peer *orientation* are different. Peer orientation is damaging and unnatural because the peer becomes a substitute parent. The teen no longer looks to Mom and

Dad for guidance. Peer orientation also sabotages the context for parenting our teens. We lose our power to shepherd our teens because we've lost their hearts.

How can you tell if your teen is peer-oriented and not just peer-attached? If your teen spends time with friends but still relies on you for guidance, if she still sees you as her best bet for getting her needs met, this is a positive sign that she enjoys peer friendships but is primarily attached to you. If your teen can hold on to her sense of self while she's with her peers, you can rest easy. On the other hand, if your teen spends time with friends and comes home talking, walking, and dressing like them, you might have a problem, particularly if your teen seems to tune you out while tuning in to anything the peers say. If your teen can't seem to maintain her own feelings, values, and boundaries when she's with her peers, ensure you are around during her peer socializing. For all teens, whether or not they are peer-oriented, don't feel guilty about de-emphasizing peer relationships. Allow some socializing, but take responsibility for keeping your teen's heart safe.

In the next chapter, we're going to take a look at Dr. Neufeld's roots of attachment: the six ways your teen attaches to you. You'll learn how you can use those six roots to engage your teen's attachment instincts and even lead your teen closer to God!

Reflection and Direction

- When parents were peer-oriented as teens, they are far more likely to accommodate or even encourage it in their own children. Reflect on your own adolescence. What role did peers have in your world? Did you look to them to meet your emotional needs? How did these experiences impact your self-perception and maturity? Have those early experiences impacted how you view the role of peers in your children's lives?

- Read Isaiah 41:13. Sit in prayer, reflecting on this short passage. How do you feel when you read God's promise to hold your hand and help you through your fears? Do you believe it? If so, thank God for his tender care for you. If you feel a lingering doubt that God will be there for you, know you are not alone. You can acknowledge this doubt or pain while deciding to move forward in your relationship with God.
- Write down a description of how you believe God feels and thinks about you. What experiences in your life led you to feel this way?

2
Anchoring Your Teen in Love and Faith

Why, even the hairs of your head are all numbered.
Fear not; you are of more value than many sparrows.
— LUKE 12:7

The Big Picture

- How to nourish your teen's faith by nurturing his attachment yearnings
- Why your teen must find his "I" with God before he can be a "we" with peers

After learning about attachment and human thriving, and especially the role of secure attachment in faith development, you might be feeling a bit overwhelmed. This is how I felt when I first received information about attachment but lacked practical ideas for how to nurture secure attachment in my home, especially given my own struggles with attachment. I gained increasing confidence as a mother as I gleaned ideas from other mothers and different parenting books. My confidence was bolstered in particular by what I learned from Dr. Neufeld about the nature of attachment and how it unfolds in childhood.

I learned that humans have one drive to attach but, as I suggested in the previous chapter, six ways of attaching. This insight transformed the way I see my children. These six roots of attachment are, according to Dr. Neufeld: physical proximity, sameness, belonging, significance, love, and being known. An infant can attach to a parent only through physical proximity, but as he matures, he becomes capable of attaching in increasingly deeper ways. Around age one year, he becomes capable of attaching through a sense of sameness to his parents. Around age two, he becomes capable of attaching through a sense of belonging and loyalty, and so on. If all goes well, a child can move through the six phases with his primary attachment figure one phase at a time during the first six years of life so that, by age six or seven, he becomes capable of attaching in all six ways. The attachment roots are relevant in all our attachment relationships from birth to death, but ideally the roots are nourished and strengthened in early childhood. When I recognized the six roots, a window opened as I sought to build healthy attachments in my home. I was able to look for ways to nurture these roots in my children's relationship with me and even their relationship with God.

Let's take a look at these six ways our kids seek to have their attachment needs met. You're interested in teens, but it's useful to understand how attachment takes root in these different modes in early childhood, so I'll frame how each of these attachment capacities develops in young children first before I share how you can meet these needs in your teenager. I'll also share some thoughts about how you can use your knowledge of the six roots of attachment to help your teen deepen his relationship with God. In many ways, attachment provides a stabilizing anchor in your teen's journey through the stages of faith that we explored in the last chapter.

1. Proximity (Being With)

Infants can attach only through the five senses. They want to see, feel, hear, and smell their attachment figures.[1] This is the most foundational way humans attach, but we should become capable of attaching in other ways as we mature. During times of crisis, or even when we are just having a hard day, we'll tend to revert to this attachment root. We just want to be near the people we love. We nourish this attachment root by showing our children with a warm and welcoming demeanor that we like to be around them. This warm invitation is so critical in our relationship with our teenagers. They are sometimes filled with self-doubt; they are often uncomfortable in their own skin. When they receive a signal from us that we enjoy their company, it soothes these self-doubts and anxieties.

Young children can feel threatened and frightened when they sense their parents don't want to be around them or the parents explicitly threaten to abandon them if they don't behave properly. A message like "If you don't come right now, I'm leaving you here" will set off separation alarm in young children. Most developmentalists discourage using time-outs with children younger than six because, at their stage of cognitive development, they can't really reflect on the consequences of their actions in a way the parent is imagining. The child experiences the time-out as a rejection, not an opportunity for self-reflection. Older kids and teens can handle being sent to their rooms to cool off or spend time alone reflecting, as long as we frame it in an attachment-protective way. For example, instead of the "get out of my sight" message, we can say that we both need space: "I think we both need some time alone so we can talk more respectfully and productively; let's take a breather."

Some practical ways to connect with teenagers through proximity include working on a project together, playing games and sports, cooking together, going on hikes, camping, or training for a race together. My husband and teenage daughter, Claire, worked side-by-side for several months repainting her room. They played music while scraping off wallpaper, repairing walls, ripping off old baseboards, and, finally, painting. I helped Claire redecorate. We had fun perusing shops to find the perfect accessories for her new, more grown-up space.

I've discovered a surprising way to invite connection to my teens through proximity: driving alone with them. I never planned it, but it seems they let their guards down when we're side by side without other kids around. I first discovered this with my oldest child, Aidan. Every Tuesday night, he and I drove alone about forty minutes away from our house to his Civil Air Patrol meetings. During those drives, he asked questions and posed topics that he never brought up when his siblings were around. We talked about all sorts of random things, including how you know you're in love, how to handle friction in friendships, and even the elements a prosecutor must prove to a jury to win a murder conviction! Lately, I enjoy car rides with my two middle children, who are now teens. So far, neither teen has been interested in murder trials, but I'm ready for anything!

Sharing a meal with or feeding your teenager is another

great way to prime her attachment to you. For all of us, eating with somebody tends to satisfy the yearning for proximity; it's an intimacy that involves seeing, touching, tasting, hearing, and smelling. We know intuitively that sharing food invites physical closeness and trust. Think of the way you ate with your spouse in the early stages of your relationship. It is an under-appreciated yet natural avenue for nurturing love in our homes. So, when your teen is having a bad day, or you simply want to reconnect, try inviting her to sit down for her favorite dessert. If my teenagers let me feed them, I know their hearts are still soft even when they're having a crummy day.

When teens sense their parents don't like being around them, they will turn to peers or other substitute attachments (like animals or objects) to get this need met. Don't be too concerned if your teen's interest in spending time with friends intensifies over the next few years. They're testing their wings as they prepare to fly your nest. What is not healthy is when your teen shuts you out while inviting the peers in. As I explained in the previous chapter, it's natural for teens to be attached to peers, but the peers should not replace you as the primary attachment figure in your teen's life.

Encountering Christ

Sometimes I imagine what it was like for the disciples who hung out with Jesus doing ordinary things. They ate with Jesus; they probably knew his favorite foods. They saw him yawn and heard him cough. They knew what his feet looked like after a long day walking through dusty streets. I would love to know Jesus that intimately. But we can still encounter Jesus; he still draws close to us. Before his ascension, Jesus promised he would not abandon his disciples, including us: "When his visible presence was taken from them, Jesus did not leave his disciples orphans. He promised to remain with them until the end of time; he sent them his

Spirit. As a result communion with Jesus has become, in a way, more intense" (CCC 788). How about that? Because we have his Spirit, our communing with him is even more intense than it was for those first disciples.

Jesus Christ established the Church and the sacraments partly because we are physical beings who experience reality through our bodies. The Church is the Body of Christ visible in the world. We gather with other believers at Mass not only because we like to see our friends but because we encounter Jesus. The sacraments are physical signs of invisible graces. God has even given us particular physical objects through which he transmits graces in the sacraments.[2] Think of anointing oil, candles, vessels, even the priest's hands. Jesus gave us these things because he understands our nature; we experience the world through our five senses, so he communicates himself and his graces through our five senses.

He promised he would be present to us, but he didn't promise that we'd have a Red Bull moment every time we pray or go to Mass. We lose many of our young people today because they expect to be stimulated and entertained passively and constantly. They may assume something isn't valuable if it isn't immediately arresting and provocative. We can gently remind our teens that many valuable things in life aren't exciting all day, every day. Major league ball players don't always feel excited; the President doesn't feel pumped about his job every minute of the day. While we hope our teens do experience moments of spiritual consolation at Mass and during prayer, they have to grow to a place where they remain faithful despite their feelings. We can remind them that Christ's promises are more reliable than human emotions, and Jesus promised, "I am with you always, to the close of the age" (Mt 28:20). Whether they *feel* God's presence or *believe* that God is present does not negate the reality that God is indeed present to them. God is being itself; he is more present to us than we can fathom.

Here are some suggestions for creating opportunities for your teen to become more aware of God's presence. First, you can lead your teen in imaginative prayer, a centuries-old practice where we place ourselves in scenes from the Gospels. We use our senses and imaginations to become an intimate part of Jesus' life, allowing him to reveal himself to us, deepening our friendship with him. We visualize ourselves in the story, noticing our physical and emotional responses. You can include your whole family in this prayer practice. Here are the basic steps:

- Pick a lively scene from the Gospels. You can usually use the daily Mass readings.
- Explain to your kids that your family will get to know Jesus better by imagining yourselves in a Bible story.
- Ask your children to close their eyes. Spend a minute in silence. Then read the passage slowly and reverently.
- Tell your kids that you're going to read the story again. But, this time, they should place themselves in the story. They might be one of the disciples or a guest. Ask them to allow God to lead them in the story. What do they see, smell, hear, and feel? What are the voices like? What objects do they notice?
- Read the story again. After you've finished reading, allow your children to sit in silence for a few minutes.
- Ask your children to share their experiences during the prayer. What did they notice? Did anybody in the scene talk to them? Did anything surprise them? What might God be saying to them through these experiences?

If a story seems particularly fruitful for your family's imaginative prayer, come back to it again the next time you pray together. If you'd like to see examples of the fruits of imaginative prayer, Creighton University has a series of imaginative prayer reflections.[3]

Second, you can share with your teens a love for the Real Presence in the Eucharist. All of the sacraments have evangelizing power, but the Eucharist is the source and summit of our lives as Catholics.[4] Jesus Christ is truly present in the Eucharist at Mass and during adoration. This is a radical self-offering to us: Jesus Christ offers himself to us, Body and Blood, Soul and Divinity. *The Bishop of the Abandoned Tabernacle* is a lovely little book to read aloud to your children and teens. It tells the true story of St. Manuel Gonzalez Garcia and his devotion to the Real Presence. As a new priest, he arrived at his first parish assignment and discovered the tabernacle covered in cobwebs and wholly neglected. Jesus was there, with only spiders as company. The rest of the parish building was in equal disrepair, and the parishioners didn't seem to care. Saint Manuel considered asking for a new assignment, but he couldn't leave Jesus in such a state. The tabernacle became the focus of his spiritual life. His words pierce our hearts and ignite our longing to keep Christ company, too:

> If Jesus is present in the tabernacle with his eyes looking at me, then when I am before him, I should be looking at the sacred Host with my physical eyes as well as with the eyes of my soul — looking into the interior of that Host. If Jesus is in the tabernacle with his ears ever ready to listen to me, then I should go before the tabernacle listening to him with all my attention, and with much interest to talk to him. If Jesus is present in the tabernacle with his hands full of gifts for the needy who come

to ask for those gifts, I should go before him with my
poverty fully exposed with great trust.[5]

2. Sameness (Being Like; Emulating)

At about age one, children begin to walk. While this is exciting
for them, it's also alarming because they can walk away from us.
Now they can't be with us physically all the time because they
want to explore and practice their walking. So, they become
capable of holding on to us — feeling close to us — by recognizing how they are like us. Here, Dr. Neufeld draws upon the
social learning theory of Dr. Albert Bandura, who observed that
we emulate those to whom we are attached. This yearning for
sameness with their attachment figures allows small children
to acquire language, values, and culture from their parents. Our
young children love to copy everything we do! They read the
newspaper with their legs crossed, wear a red baseball cap to
clean the yard, tap their finger on the table — your child feels
connected to you by doing what you do, noticing how he looks
and acts like you, and even eating what you eat. It's adorable! It's
also completely healthy for small children to want to imitate you
like this. This impulse to imitate our attachment figures is wired
into us; it is not weird. It's a way our children hold on to us even
when they can't be with us; it reduces separation alarm. In fact,
their ability to imitate us forms their core identity. We identify
with the roles, traditions, and characteristics of our attachment
figures and that identification shapes our personalities.

You and your teen don't have exactly the same tastes and
interests, and he knows it. But it's still helpful to emphasize the
things you do both like and how you are similar. I have a few tips
for nurturing this attachment root with teens:

- Emphasize shared hobbies. Do you and your teen
  both like fishing, music, or gaming? Are you both

curious about archery or medieval castles?

- Step outside your comfort zone and explore things that interest your teen, even if you've never been particularly interested.
- Emphasize family rituals and traditions, which form the basis of family culture and a foundation for your child's life narrative. In adulthood, we often reminisce about the things we did when we were little that made our family an "us." Even if your teen seems to be drifting mentally away from you toward his future, don't stop creating that cultural foundation for him.
- When your teen is struggling with a personal conflict, empathize and share your own experience. "Yeah, that happened to me once, and it was awful"; "I sometimes can't sleep the night before a big event either." You're supporting your teen and helping him feel that you're in the same boat.

When kids feel like they and their parents live in different universes because they have nothing in common, they often turn to peers for a sense of sameness. They look to their peers for cues about how to dress and talk and what to value. In fact, this is the default attachment mode for most teenagers in the West today. We assume they are meant to be like their peers, but they are meant to be like us. It is our culture, values, and traditions that help our teens navigate the pitfalls of adolescence. So, it's our responsibility to hold on to them and make it safe to depend on us.

In our work of evangelizing our children, it's useful to recognize that discipleship and imitation are linked. God taps into this intuition in us to imitate our attachment figures. In first-century Judaism, discipleship was all about imitation: living with the teacher; eating, praying, and studying with him. This is how

Jesus led his disciples. They learned how to be, what to do, and what to believe by observing Christ as he worked, prayed, and played. The Church emerged and grew by passing on the Deposit of Faith through a chain of relationships from one generation to the next. And that is how we are to evangelize our children. If our children are attached to us, they will watch us at work, play, and prayer, and they will learn what to do, when, and why. We want our kids to imitate us and follow us so that we can lead them to Christ. If our children are called to marriage, we hope they will pass on to the next generation what they received from us.

Imitating Real Heroes

Teens are looking for heroes to emulate. Their heroes give them a vision of what they might become and what greatness looks like in action. Where do our kids look for heroes today? Too often, they make heroes out of reality stars, pop stars, and social media influencers — rarely people worth modeling their lives after. Many teens spend hours a day studying these false heroes.

We can ensure our teens have real heroes in their midst and know what sort of people are worth admiring. Have a casual conversation with your teen about how they would define a hero, then invite her to explore some great heroes with you. You can start with saints' lives and Bible stories. Are they named after a saint? Do they have a confirmation saint? What virtues do these saints exhibit? What sacrifices did they make for their faith? You might begin with St. Thomas More, who held fast to his moral convictions in the face of public pressure — a familiar conflict to many teens. More possessed extraordinary integrity; he refused to cross a line that he knew shouldn't be crossed, even when it cost him everything, including his life. Many men and women in the Bible exhibit exceptional courage and trust in God in the face of danger. You can find decent films about many saints and biblical heroes that may pique your teen's interest.[6]

Classic literature like *The Aeneid, To Kill a Mockingbird, The Hobbit,* or *Robin Hood* and movies based on them can provide opportunities to explore heroism with your teen. What makes the protagonists heroes? Does your teen admire these characters or have reservations about their actions? Your teen might identify with reluctant heroes like Bilbo Baggins in *The Hobbit,* who doubts his readiness for "an adventure" but steps forward anyway.

Of course, don't overlook the ordinary men and women around you who have qualities worth emulating. Point out to your children the heroism of grandparents, aunts, uncles, priests, police officers, firefighters, and other public servants. And let's not forget the greatest hero of all: Jesus Christ! While other heroes fight human foes, often to win their own glory, Jesus fought and conquered sin and death, emptying himself completely to win our redemption.

3. Belonging (Loyalty; Belonging With)

While we have some things in common with them, at age two or three our kids notice the many ways they are different from us. They experience this difference as a kind of separation, but now they become capable of feeling close to us through a sense of belonging and loyalty. Toddlers claim their parents ("He's MY daddy!"), and they love to be claimed ("my girl" or "my little buddy"). You will notice them drawing family groups; they have a developing sense that cousins, grandparents, and other extended family belong in their family. They love to hear reminders that they belong with us and that we are on their side.

Whatever their ages, whether they are our children by birth or adoption, our children enjoy hearing the stories of how they became part of our family: how we waited for them, chose their names, and welcomed them home. If possible, we can pass on to them the stories of the people, places, and objects from our family history. Most families have love stories, war stories, and stories about heirlooms and other objects. Kids seem particularly fascinated by stories about family surnames. My family on both my maternal and paternal sides come from Scandinavia; I have a partial family tree going back several generations. My children were delighted to learn the names of some of these ancestors, especially Magnusson and Magnusdotter, which mean "son of the Great" and "daughter of the Great." Who was Magnus, anyway, and what made him great? I'll probably never know, but I wonder about it with my children, and the name provides an opportunity to talk about what being "great" means in the eyes of our Lord, Jesus Christ, who was great because of his self-giving love and sacrifice. Even if you don't know a lot of your family history, share what little you know so your kids feel part of a story that began long before they were born.

This attachment yearning is also about loyalty — knowing that our family has our back through thick and thin. Teens are in the thick of it. As they negotiate the challenges and changes of adolescence, they experience bad days, relationship fractures, and stumbles. So, adolescence is a critical time to protect this attachment root. Usually, our teens don't need us to fix their problems for them; they just need to know we are on their side, offering support and encouragement. For example, when my teens are frazzled about meeting assignment deadlines for school, I can't take over and do the homework for them, but I often fold their laundry for them, bring them surprise snacks (feeding!), and just sit with them while they vent. Sometimes our teens won't want to talk about what's bothering them, but we can still nourish attachment by being available to them.

Belonging must be unconditional. If our teens sense that our loyalty to them is fragile, their separation alarm goes off. If their belonging with us is contingent on their performance or behavior, they do not feel safe in the relationship. They may perform and behave, but they may not thrive. Remember: Our children mature from a place of rest. If they are preoccupied with pursuing and maintaining a fragile attachment, they will not leave the safe harbor of the relationship to explore and take healthy risks. We must remind our kids during a conflict that they still belong with us. We can set and enforce firm boundaries on behavior while making it clear that our kids always belong with us, even when we hit rough patches. We can correct our kids' behavior while reminding them that they are still our kids, and we love them. We can also be loyal to them without sorting out their squabbles with siblings and friends. Basically, we want our teens to know that nothing they do will ever sever our love or the relationship. This seems simple, but the simple things are often missing in our closest relationships, which is undoubtedly true in many parent-teen relationships.

Belonging and Forgiveness

When our teens feel our invitation and affirmation that they belong with us, we are being Christ to them. In particular, when we make it clear that our teens belong with us even when they mess up, we create the foundation for our teens' relationship with Christ, who always invites them back when they walk away. Especially as teenagers launch from our nests, we want them to know what to do when they fail morally. When they stumble, they can run into God's arms; they need not fear him. Through the Sacrament of Reconciliation, they are restored and reconciled to God and his Church.

When Jesus spoke about sin, his message was about "metanoia" — a conversion, a change of mind and heart.[7] He asks us to turn toward him, toward home, toward a new way of thinking and living. Jesus demonstrates metanoia in the parable of the prodigal son (see Lk 15:11–32). A much-loved son leaves his family behind and descends into debauchery, eventually losing everything. Returning home with regret and humility, he asks to work as a hired hand for his father because he feels so unworthy. His father not only welcomes him home, but he wraps his son in a fine robe and throws him a lavish feast. Because of Christ, the great bridge between heaven and earth, between Father and failure, there is always room for us in God's house at his great table. When we are willing to let go of control and allow God to enter

---

Only Humans Can Attach Deeply

All mammals with a limbic system are capable of attaching through these first three levels of attachment (proximity, sameness, and belonging), but only humans can attach through the last three phases (significance, emotional intimacy, and psychological intimacy). The first three require less vulnerability and emotional maturity than the latter three. In fact, most people with severe emotional issues or attachment wounds struggle to attach through the latter three attachment roots.

Teen friendships usually involve some attempt at closeness at the first three levels of attachment. They feel close only if they are physically with and exactly the same as each other. Their sense of "belonging" is often tribalistic and possessive; it is not the true belonging that human beings long for and need. Teen friendships are marked by anxiety and instability because of the superficial way they attach to each other. A peer can abruptly send a message that our teen does not belong anymore, usually over things that seem innocuous to us. Having a warm relationship with a parent is so important for helping teens navigate these inevitable losses in peer friendships.

---

the chaos we often create in our lives, our minds and hearts can be changed. We always belong, if we are willing to return home and take our place at the banquet table. *We* have to believe this if our teens are to believe it.

If you don't already have one, institute a family routine of going to confession. For example, have a particular day or weekend when you always go to confession together. Before you go, remind your kids that the purpose of confession isn't to scare us but to restore our relationship with God. Confession gives us the graces we need to resist sin and build healthy relationships with others, including God. If you struggle with confession or you're concerned you don't understand it well enough to talk about it with your kids, you might look at Good Catholic's YouTube series on confession.

4. Significance (To Count; To Be Cherished)

At age three or four, children become capable of attaching through a sense of significance: They feel connected to the people who hold them dear. Developmental psychologist Urie Bronfenbrenner famously said that "every child needs at least one adult who is irrationally crazy about them."[8] (Notice, the child needs an adult, not a peer — or a cat!) Kids thirst for this deep regard. Our kids need to be able to take for granted that we cherish them deeply. We nourish this attachment root by giving our kids our soft, warm eyes when we look at them, by noticing their interests, their moods, their opinions. We must give our children this regard as a gift; we must not make them win it or earn it. After all, this is the way God loves us.

One of the most powerful ways to nurture this root with teens is by prioritizing time with them. Many parents back out of their relationship with their kids in the teen years; they assume the teen doesn't want them anymore. Teens still yearn for a secure attachment to their parents even if some of them put up a cool front. So, with little kids, you can make a big stink about them when they walk in the room, and you can hang up their poems on the fridge to show them how much they matter; they seem to feed on this attention. With some teens, you need a subtler touch. Just show up, especially teens you say you'll be there. Show up to their games, volunteer for their scouting troop, be there for family game night. A faith bonus: The Fuller Youth Institute found that when parents prioritize both planned and spontaneous time with their teens, the teens are more likely to continue practicing their faith as young adults.[9] By the way, you can still make a big stink about your teen when he walks in the room, and you can hang up his poems on the fridge! Even if he doesn't flash you a toothy grin, he probably still appreciates your attention and regard.

One small gesture I make with my teens to nourish this attachment root: Every night before bed, I seek them out to connect with them briefly in private. Sometimes teenagers are overlooked in the nighttime routine as we deal with the more urgent needs of smaller kids, so I make a point to remember my big kids. Nothing complicated. Sometimes this exchange takes five seconds; at other times, they want to bend my ear. Another idea: Institute gratitude rituals during family meetings or at the dinner table. Ask each person to share how God has blessed them that day and take this opportunity to thank God for your children. Mention each of them by name and thank God for the things about them that you appreciate.

We can make a point of helping our teens find ways to identify, explore, and use their gifts and talents. One of the tasks of adolescence is to recognize how God has put us together uniquely for a reason; he has given us what we need to fulfill our holy mission on earth. Our teens might have a mission that escapes our radar because their skills, talents, and temperament differ from ours. At more superficial attachment levels, our kids can feel anxious about these differences, but we can show them that we enjoy witnessing the unfolding of their many gifts. For example, my daughters are very artistic. Even in early elementary school, they were both better artists than I ever was or could be. I never felt much inclined to pursue art, other than sewing projects, but I ask questions about their art projects and show them how much I enjoy and value their artistic gifts by displaying their work on the walls in our home.

Wanting to matter to somebody requires much greater vulnerability than being the same as them or sitting next to them. Our children take a risk when they allow themselves to feel this yearning to matter to us, to be dear to us. Our challenge is to remain the answer to their need to matter. If they believe they don't matter to us, or if our regard for them is conditional, they may revert to more superficial ways of attaching to us — these more superficial ways are the first three roots of attachment. So they obsess about being the same as us, or they become clingy. Or they may become emotionally defended against caring what we think, seeking instead to matter to peers or online contacts who can never fulfill their attachment needs.

As our teens begin to explore who they are and why they matter, we want them to base their sense of significance on the truth and a stable foundation. If they believe they matter only when they win, if they're popular, or because they are the pitcher on the baseball team, their sense of mattering is precarious. In reality, they matter because they are priceless children of God, made in his image and made for a mission with transcendent value. We want to leave our teens without a doubt that they are valuable because of who they are and not for what they do or achieve. Ultimately, we want them to feel in their gut how much they matter to God. He is crazy about them. More, they are icons of a God who holds the universe in existence. Our children's

significance springs from this paradox: They are utterly dependent on God for their existence, and he treasures them uniquely
among his creation.

Parishes That Value Teens

Recall that in the affiliative faith stage, our teens want to feel
valued by their faith communities. It's great if they connect with
their peers at our parishes, but it's most important that they feel
appreciated by adult members and leaders. The Fuller Youth
Institute looked at thirteen activities common in church youth
groups. They found the strongest contributor to mature faith in
teens and young adults is their exposure to intergenerational
faith groups at their churches.[10] (The Institute identified other
effective activities, including service projects and retreats, which
I'll address in a later chapter.) Not good snacks in the youth
room. Not guitars at Mass. Not a youth minister who's relatable
and stylish. No: intergenerational faith relationships. Dr. Neufeld
has been making this point for decades in the secular arena: To
thrive emotionally and socially, our kids desperately need to be
embedded in caring, hierarchical relationships. They need the
same thing to thrive spiritually. In chapter four, I'll talk more
about intergenerational faith experiences and your teen's friendships with caring adults.

5. Love (Emotional Intimacy)

When conditions are right, at about age four or five, kids can
move forward into a very tender stage of attachment. They become capable of endearing, soft expressions of feelings. They
want to give their hearts away. Here is the beginning of emotional intimacy, which requires great vulnerability and trust. When
our children attach at the heart, they are yearning for a "forever"
relationship. They want to hold on to us forever and want us to
hold on to them. Small kids might say they're going to marry you

or live with you forever. We know logically this won't happen, but we can nurture this attachment root by assuring them that we will be their mommy or daddy forever, and they can live with us as long as they want. (Of course, by the time they're fifteen, they'll have other plans!)

One of the critical ways we nourish this attachment root with our teenagers is by making it safe for them to express their emotions. In *Discipleship Parenting*, I discuss the importance of making room for all our children's emotions, not just the ones we prefer to see.[11] If we aren't comfortable with all their emotions, our kids won't be either. And they may believe that some of their emotions are bad. "Children need to become comfortable experiencing the full array of their emotions, because their emotions help them become integrated human beings. Emotions aren't something to fear, avoid, or eradicate."[12] While we can surely guide our teens in expressing their emotions respectfully, we should never shame them for having emotions. Emotions are natural and automatic internal responses to stimuli; they just happen to us without our control, like an itch or a hiccup. The *expression* of emotions can be sinful, but emotions are not sinful. Unlike an itch or a hiccup, our emotional reactions can be tempered through the cultivation of virtue and the integration of our emotions with our wills. As the Catechism explains, "In themselves passions are neither good nor evil. They are morally qualified only to the extent that they effectively engage reason and will" (CCC 1767). We can be matter-of-fact about having emotions while mentoring our teens in expressing their emotions appropriately. We can help our teens identify the virtue missing in inappropriate emotional expressions and teach them to use their emotions for good. They will mess up a lot, like we do. We can all begin again.

I am not suggesting that our kids' feelings are reflective of reality or truth. One of the missteps in modern psychological theory is the assumption that mental health requires that feelings be expressed and affirmed, whatever they are, even when the feelings are expressed in a socially harmful way, even when the feelings don't reflect reality, and even when the feelings change from one minute to the next! There is a difference between affirming that an emotion exists and believing that it reflects the truth. Often we feel a certain way because we've misjudged others or situations. It doesn't mean our feelings should be ignored, but they shouldn't receive priority over reason.

Dr. Neufeld calls emotional intimacy the "long arm of attachment" because it is so powerful. When our children attach to us at the heart, they will have the courage to stretch their wings farther away from home; they can bear separation for greater distances and more prolonged periods because they're able to carry our love and a sense of home with them. When our kids are attached to us at the heart, they can hold on to us through arguments, illnesses, or other types of serious separation. Teenagers need safe adults to protect their hearts. The world is a wounding and toxic place, especially the world of teens today. When we protect them emotionally, when we remain their answer, their hearts remain soft even when they face teasing or rejection from their peers. When they feel held by us emotionally, the attachment gives them strength and courage; they are not as impacted by what the peers think and do because they haven't given their hearts to the peers.

Without the capacity to attach to us through emotional intimacy, our teens will revert to more shallow forms of attachment, or they will give their hearts to people who aren't safe. Healthy adults tend to self-select for people who are emotionally whole; they know intuitively that their emotions are safe in such relationships. They also never give their hearts away to new friends; they move through the proximity, sameness, belonging, and significance stages in the relationship before they are ready to share from the heart. In contrast, anxiously attached adults often bare their souls to people they hardly know; they lack boundaries. Teenagers often have the same problem by nature of their immaturity; they wear their hearts on their sleeves to prove that they trust each other. So often this trust is misplaced, and rarely can a peer handle our teens' most tender emotions. When teenagers are promiscuous, they are *always* trying to manufacture emotional intimacy with a peer — they are offering the most vulnerable part of themselves to somebody who is too immature to handle it.

Our teens are meant to give their hearts to their parents, siblings, grandparents — the people who will treasure their hearts and protect them until they grow up.

The God Who Adores Teens

God is crazy about our teenagers. How do we convince them of this? First, by modeling it. Setting aside our own needs and interests to care for them, listen to them, and celebrate them; readily forgiving them and recognizing their good intentions when they blow it; making room in our lives for the things they care about: These things create a foundation for our teens as they begin making a more personal connection to God in the searching faith stage. We also model by mentioning ways God has shown up for us, and how we ourselves discern God's love in our lives. Talk to your teen at some point about what it means to be chosen and adored. Ask your teen whether she's ever been left off a guest list for a party or overlooked when teams are being picked in sports. Well, God always invites her; he always chooses her.

When our children feel loved by us unconditionally, as imperfect as we are at it, they can understand better how God could love them unconditionally. God's love does not depend on their grades, their popularity, or even their virtue. Even when they are downright nasty, God still loves them. God doesn't wait for them to shape up before he loves them. Their friends and even we will fail to love them perfectly, but God's love is perfect. He shows up and will not leave their side, even when they refuse to love him back. They can unload on him and be honest about their feelings. They can't convince him to stop loving them. He loves them so much, he will give everything for them, even his own life:

> While we were still helpless, at the right time Christ died for the ungodly. Why, one will hardly die for a righteous man — though perhaps for a good man one will dare even to die. But God shows his love for us in that while we were yet sinners Christ died for us. (Romans 5:6–8)

6. Being Known (Psychological Intimacy)

Finally, at around age five or six, children become capable of psychological intimacy. They realize they have thoughts their parents don't know about. They experience this privacy as a kind of separation (though they also find it very exciting). Children will tend to share their secrets, ideas, and other thoughts with their attachment figure quite naturally, if they feel safe. They enjoy private chats and personal sharing. This is part of the attachment dance. As they reveal themselves to us, we can become the answer to what they need, and we can understand them better.

Teenagers are very different from young children when it comes to personal sharing. While they need to have a safe person to talk to about their ideas, concerns, and dreams, they also begin to want a private interior world. Both of these inclinations (for psychological intimacy and privacy) exist in them, and it's very healthy. Your teen shouldn't be deceptive and sneaky, and you should see some transparency, but sometimes he'll need mental space to work things out for himself, which is marvelous. So, don't be too concerned if your teen doesn't share as much as he did when he was little.

We hope our teens will talk to us when they feel burdened by ethical questions, peer conflicts, and academic stress, but sometimes we make it hard for them. With all the tips we get about communicating with our teenagers, you'd think we'd be experts, but nope. We immediately interrupt them with advice or interrogation! When my teens start telling me something that surprises or scares me, I have to consciously resist my tendency to freak out and control the situation. I tell myself, "Just. Be. Quiet. LISTEN." I know my teens are testing the waters initially to see how I react. If the waters are safe, they will wade in a little farther and continue talking. Safe doesn't mean I always like what they're saying, but I try to make it clear that I am on their side and I care.

Psychological intimacy is about transparency and being deeply known. We don't experience this closeness with very many people. Some teenagers want to force this closeness with a peer. Teenagers sometimes tell their "secrets" to each other because they want to prove they trust each other. I think this is particularly true for girls. Too often this trust is misplaced. Our teenagers can find themselves betrayed and hurt. Our teens may also try to get their emotional needs met on social media. Psychological intimacy has nothing to do with posting about ourselves on the internet. In fact, social media sharing is a form of depersonalized intimacy; it's a façade of closeness. As long as we understand this, it's not a problem, but most teens don't understand this. If they use social media as their primary way of sharing themselves, they are not experiencing fulfilling friendships. So, we can take the lead and interrupt this tendency to isolate behind technology and social media platforms.

"NO T.O.T.T. Nights"

When our teens express their doubts and questions about God or the Church, particularly during the searching faith stage, they're trusting us to help them. We want to reassure our teens that they still belong with us and in the Church even when they have doubts and ask hard questions. We can connect our teens to God at these moments by pointing out that 1) God already knows about their doubts and 2) God wants to hear their true feelings and thoughts, not what they think God wants them to feel and think. One great idea to nurture this attachment root: Set aside special nights (or mornings or afternoons) when your teen can ask all her hard questions about God. I call them "NO T.O.T.T." nights, which stands for "no topic off the table" nights, but it also means no small kids are around interrupting the teen's train of thought or the parent's answer. In your home, this may mean one parent and the teen go to a coffee shop for privacy while the other parent covers the little kids back home.

Make it special, and come prepared! Teens tend to ask very predictable questions, but most modern Catholic parents can't answer them because we were so poorly catechized. (Hand raised here.) So as part of our own growth as disciple parents responsible for shepherding our children, we get to put ourselves through self-study apologetics school. (I'm kidding ... sort of.) I have a few resources to get you started. If your teen has basic questions about Church teaching, I like Trent Horn's *Why We're Catholic*; you can read this book with your teen. If your teen seems to be wondering about the Church's position on moral issues, check out *Made This Way: How to Prepare Kids to Face Today's Tough Moral Issues* by Leila Miller and Trent Horn, which offers age-appropriate responses to kids' questions on a variety of difficult topics, including abortion, homosexuality, transgenderism, and premarital sex. *Tough Choices: Bringing Moral Choices Home* by Sean Lynch presents moral dilemmas to discuss with your kids, accompanied by explanations of the Church teaching related to the dilemmas. Father Mike Schmitz's YouTube videos are a great resource to share with your teens. He doesn't mess around when it comes to sharing the truth, but he also presents Church teaching with a compassionate tone. I like *Quick Catholic Lessons with Fr. Mike*, which gives you discussion questions, activities, and prayers to go with several of his videos, so you can create a whole mini-retreat type experience with your teen!

You can also arrange "NO T.O.T.T." nights with other teens and a well-prepared parish priest or youth leader, but I do think it's vital that parents do something like this alone with their teens occasionally, too. We want them to know that we welcome their questions, even if we need a few days to answer them. Invite your teen to search for answers with you! Show her how the Catechism is divided into topical sections; share some of your favorite faith resources with her so she can take the initiative to look up answers to her questions. Inevitably, there will be some questions that we can't answer — perhaps it exceeds the limits of our understanding, or it's unanswerable right now. In those moments, I remind my teens that sometimes there is a lesson in the wondering or the waiting.

The God Who Knows Teens
One of the heartbreaks of adolescence is that our teens realize we will never completely understand them. Eventually, they learn that every friend and loved one, at some point, will blow it and fail to understand what they need and who they are. If our deepest human longing is for perfect psychological intimacy — for somebody to get us one hundred percent, 24/7 — we will never experience it in our human relationships. Human companionship is necessary for a fulfilling journey through life, but it always involves some disconnections and disappointments.

We sometimes learn more about ourselves in these relation-ships than the other person learns about us. We learn about our unrealistic expectations, our blind spots, our pride — the things that create cracks in human connection.

In reality, only God can perfectly meet our longing to be understood and known. We want our teenagers to know that God knows the whole truth about them — he knows the em-barrassing, dumb things they do in secret; he knows the dark parts of them they want to tuck away in a corner. He knows them, and he still wants and loves them. He wants them to love him back. "But you, O LORD, know me; / you see me, and test my mind toward you." (Jer 12:3a). He also wants them to share ev-erything with him, including their sufferings and failures. They don't need to hold anything back for fear that God can't handle it. What's more, God will make something beautiful from their hurts. "The lives of the faithful, their praise, sufferings, prayer, and work, are united with those of Christ and with his total offering, and so acquire a new value. Christ's sacrifice present on the altar makes it possible for all generations of Christians to be united with his offering" (CCC 1368).

As our teens' relationship with God deepens, they will begin to see how perfectly God understands who they are, what they need, and when they need it. Only God satisfies completely.

When Conditions Weren't Perfect

When explaining the process of attachment in his classes, Dr. Neufeld always uses a graphic of a tree with six tree roots labeled with the six roots of human attachment. The roots plunge down in a staggered pattern, with the first root (proximity) very near the surface of the soil, the second root (sameness) pushes down a bit deeper, and the third root (belonging) deeper still, and so on. The last three roots dig down deep in the graphic — spreading out horizontally under the ground.

A tree attached to the earth with deep roots is more stable in the wind; it is less likely to blow over or suffer damage. The same is true of humans. The more ways we have of attaching, and the more we become capable of attaching through the three deeper roots, the greater resilience we will have against the storms of life. We'll bounce back, find our bearings again, and be stronger for it.

While we carry within us the *potential* to attach in these six ways, potential and reality are two different matters. While children can potentially attach in all six ways by age six, some children take longer to develop these capacities. Even in adulthood, some of us still struggle with the most vulnerable attachment roots: emotional and psychological intimacy. The good news is that it is never too late — neither for our kids nor us. So if you see signs that your children are struggling with attachment, just be the answer to that attachment need — fill the attachment cup to overflowing, starting now. In time, you will see a shift, and they will relax more into their relationship with you.

For anybody leading teens in their faith journeys, understanding these six innate needs is a game-changer. Before we can catechize and convert, we must care for the wounded hearts of many young people walking around our homes and parishes. Seasoned missionaries know that before we can minister to anybody, we have to meet their primary needs. Teens' primary needs are not for donuts and rap music. They need to know they belong with and matter to us, and we love them and understand them. This is where we must begin in our work of evangelizing teens today. Love is the beginning and the end.

Attachment, Emergence, and Solitude

Attachment is only part of the maturing process. Developmentalists talk about two other drives that help us grow up: emergence and integration.[13] **Emergence** (also called individuation) is that drive within us to become independent, confident adults with a coherent sense of self; **integration** is a drive to take our place in society without losing our sense of separateness. As long as they are not peer-oriented, our teens are working hard on emergence, but they won't be working as much on integration until they reach late adolescence and early adulthood. So, while we possess all three drives from birth, the drives to attach and emerge are dominant during childhood and adolescence. In fact, sometimes, a child can flip between attachment and emergence rapidly in the same day or even the same hour. This kind of polarity is most common in toddlers and teenagers.[14] For example, your teen might insist on driving herself to school one morning, only to call ten minutes later crying because she got lost on the way and needs your help.

While the three drives are coexistent in humans, they do seem to build on one another somewhat sequentially. Without attachment, a person will not be emergent; without emergence, a person will not integrate well into a community or society. So, only when teens are securely attached to their parents do they have the capacity for emergence; that is, to live with vitality as they explore their beliefs, interests, and values. Only when teens are emergent are they ready to contribute to a social group and integrate into that group without disappearing. Non-emergent teens (and adults) tend to blend into a group, becoming absorbed by it without maintaining their integrity — their core self. Our teens do need opportunities to contribute to our parishes and other social groups so they can practice their social skills, explore their talents and faith, and challenge themselves outside their comfort zones, but they may struggle with a wobbly sense of self throughout adolescence, which makes real integration difficult. As long as parents are aware of this problem, they can help teens navigate group

---

Three Drives That Push Us to Grow Up

1. Attachment: capacity for connection through the six roots
2. Emergence: capacity to explore our own opinions, ideas, and aspirations
3. Integration: capacity for togetherness without the loss of separateness

---

socializing and limit it when necessary. You will see flashes of healthy integration in your teen during adolescence — moments she decides to do what is right or what she loves, despite what her friends think. The emergent teen who possesses a healthy capacity for integration can be with her peers and still be herself. She is like a raisin mixed into a batter: You can still see the raisin; the raisin is still a raisin while being part of something else. The non-emergent teen is like flour in the batter — you no longer see the flour; it is absorbed by the other ingredients.

In chapter one, I mentioned the attachment void of adolescence. At some point during the teen years, a void opens up when the teen realizes that he must eventually leave the comforts of home and make his way in the world. The void results from his increasing analytical skills and sexual maturing, and it has a critical developmental purpose. Through emergence, our teen should fill the void with his own aspirations and a sharper vision of himself as a child of God. If he sees himself only through his peers' eyes or even our eyes, he cannot see the whole truth about himself. Again, it is the emergence of a coherent sense of self that provides a sense of permanence and stability in our teens' personalities and prepares them for healthy social integration in adulthood. We will talk more about integration in a later chapter. For our purposes now, I want to underscore that our teens need to find their "I" before they can become a "we" with their peers or with a spouse later in adulthood. If they don't do the work of emergence now, they will lose their way and struggle in their relationships later. Spiritual masters have long understood this truth: We are not prepared for self-donation until we have self-possession.

Our teens find their "I" partly in the attachment dance; they sometimes depend on us, lean on us. However, at other times we step aside while they press out into the world, exploring their dreams, roles, culture, and faith. Notice that our teens don't leave attachment behind to become emergent; they are attached during emergence, and because they feel safe in the attachment, they have the courage to explore, question, and ponder who they are and where they're called to go in the world. They return to the attachment harbor regularly to recharge, readying their sails for the strong winds of emergence. So, despite the assumptions of many, teenagers are not meant to detach from the adults who are responsible for their well-being. Feel confident in inviting your teen to lean on and count on you. At some point, he'll look away from you toward his own projects and passions. Then, you get out of the way, admiring and facilitating emergence.

One way we facilitate emergence is by ensuring our teenagers have enough time alone. I can't stress enough how important this is. Solitude is essential to the emergent process. This insight in social science echoes Pope John Paul II's remarks about mankind's "original solitude" in his *Theology of the Body*.[15] What was the purpose of Adam's solitude before God created Eve? It was the basis of a "test" or "examination" in which Adam became conscious of himself set apart from the rest of creation. We must all spend time alone before God so we might come to "self-definition" and "self-knowledge."[16] Our teenagers need solitude to think, wonder, and wrestle with their big questions about themselves and the world. Solitude is not optional.

Many teens today (and adults) resist being alone with their own thoughts; they continually distract themselves with mindless amusement and noise. And peer-oriented kids absorb the thoughts, ideas, aspirations, and dreams of their peers — this is conformity, not emergence. These modern tendencies impede our teens' development. They need enough time alone, free of distractions, so the void of attachment is filled with their emerging humanity and a refined vision of their lives. The void creates longings, questions, and loneliness that turn the teen toward their own inner landscape. This is why the void, when approached with the virtues of courage and curiosity, is a gateway to God. Our teens will discover that God is the ultimate answer to all their longings, questions, and loneliness.

Encouraging Habits of Solitude

If technology, peers, and entertainment aren't helpful, what should our teens do when they're spending time alone? Stare at the ceiling? Well, this wouldn't be a terrible idea! But I would suggest two things. First, facilitate and encourage creative expression as much as possible. Make it easy for your teen to get lost in creative activities. Provide the tools they need for different projects, depending on their interests and personalities: journals, music, books, knitting, leatherwork, papermaking — these are healthy outlets for mixed emotions and exploration. When our teens can sit alone, pounding, mixing, drawing, strumming, dancing, stitching, we know they are okay. Many of their chaotic emotions can come out to play during these activities. Creative solitude is a mark of a healthy teen. More, creative expression is a form of spiritual contemplation; it teaches our teens to pay attention to the gifts of the Earth and to appreciate the spark of the Divine within them as they create.

Second, facilitate and encourage your teen's exploration of prayer, spirituality, and the Church's teachings. How this looks will depend on your teen's needs. If he is still in the early imitative faith stage and doesn't have a personal prayer life yet, or if he lacks curiosity about spiritual matters, you'll start by leading your teen in prayer, by modeling for him that God is always the source of answers to our questions. If your teen is somewhere in the affiliative and searching faith stages, he is ready for spiritual direction from you. You become like a midwife to his spiritual life, guiding and guarding while what is true, good, and real in him comes to the surface in his search for God, the source of truth, goodness, and reality.

As his spiritual director, you are helping him take ownership of his spiritual life. Allow him to create his own sacred space in your home where he can retreat for spiritual reading, meditation, and prayer. If your teen expresses an interest in adoration, make that happen. If he likes to pray in nature, get him to his favorite prayer space or let him create a prayer corner in your yard. Find apps that your teen can use to explore prayer styles. Laudate, Hallow, Amen, and Abide are apps your teen might use for prayer time. If he is interested in specific Church teachings or areas of ministry, find resources to nurture that curiosity. Again, at least some of this exploration should be done in solitude. As Catholics, we know corporate prayer and faith communities are critical to our faith development, but we all need time alone too. The crisis of faith in the searching faith stage is such an example: Our teens need wise mentors to help them through it, but they also need time alone to sort out their thoughts and questions. Even Jesus regularly went off alone to pray and reflect.[17]

Helping our teens develop the habit of contemplation and solitude will benefit them for the rest of their lives. They'll come to crave silence and retreat; they'll be more comfortable with the discipline necessary for spiritual growth and deep prayer. Even active participation at Mass requires an ability to be still and receptive to an encounter with God.[18] The purpose of solitude is not to navel-gaze but for the teen to understand himself in relationship to God and to identify his questions and where to look for good answers.

When our teens are in right relationship with God, their questions begin to change as they mature. Instead of asking, "How much money will I make here?" they ask, "Will I serve God's kingdom here?" Instead of asking, "How good does my hair look today?" they ask, "How is my heart today?" Instead of asking, "What will you do for me, God?" they ask, "How can I use my life to glorify you, God?" If our teens eventually get to these questions, they will begin to live more freely and abundantly.

In these last two chapters, we've explored how to *lead* our teens and why it's important. We've seen that our teens' sense of safety with us gives them confidence to explore their questions about themselves and their faith. Their search for meaning will lead them to heaven and sainthood if they know whom to follow. We can do a lot to shepherd our teens through the chaos of adolescence if they let us lead them. But in the end, we want them to discover that they have a greater leader waiting for them. We pray that eventually, God becomes our teens' primary attachment figure. When our teens ask themselves those vulnerable questions about God — Does God want to be near me? Do I matter to him? Do I belong with him? Does he care about and know me? — we want them to know without a doubt that God shouts, YES! God will provide the best answers to their most profound questions about the nature of reality, themselves, and their purpose in the world.

Reflection and Direction
- Reflect on the six roots of attachment: proximity (physical closeness), sameness, belonging, significance, emotional intimacy (feeling emotionally safe), and psychological intimacy (feeling known and understood). How are you feeding these attachment hungers in your relationship with your teen?
- Have you tended to overlook particular attachment roots? Why do you think this is the case? Are you uncomfortable with particular types of closeness? Make a list of ways you can work on your connec-

tion with your teen in these areas. Start with the tips
I gave in this chapter but brainstorm your own ideas
considering your teen's personality and interests.

- How did the discussion of solitude strike you? Do
  you avoid sitting alone because it makes you uncomfortable? If so, wean yourself from the distractions that make it hard for you to surrender to solitude. God wants to meet you in your solitude. He
  doesn't need you to achieve anything when you sit
  with him. He just wants to hang out with you.

Inspire

3
Questing with Your Teen on Mission

*All men and women are entrusted with the task
of crafting their own life: in a certain sense, they
are to make of it a work of art, a masterpiece.*
— POPE ST. JOHN PAUL II, LETTER TO ARTISTS

The Big Picture
- Why your teen must understand her identity before she can recognize her mission
- Why family service should not be optional

99

- Commonsense principles for justice-minded teens

Just as Christ led the first disciples toward spiritual maturity through continual invitations, so we lead our teens. *You are welcome here. Come closer. Follow me.* At some point, though, we must give our disciples (our teenagers) a chance to respond, as Christ did. If we're always talking, explaining, and inviting, but we don't leave room or time for our teens' response, they can become numb to the invitation.[1]

The time and space for self-reflection that we talked about in the last chapter give our teens a chance to respond — to think about what to do with what we are giving them. This response may come in many different forms. They may have questions; they may want to explore different prayer approaches; they may wish to visit shrines or cathedrals; they may even have a negative reaction. Our role as our teens' spiritual directors is to facilitate these experiences, and when appropriate, accompany them through their questions and struggles.

This chapter will focus on one very important response: missionary action. Christ formed his disciples by teaching them, modeling for them, and reproving them. Eventually, he sent them out on mission to give to others what he'd given to them. While our teens may not be ready to go on a mission in a big way, we can lead them in small ways toward exercising their empathy muscles and being Christ to others in the world. Now, my friends, we begin to see the fruits of discipleship parenting, the first buds bursting from those seeds planted and tended with love and patience over many years. And what if you feel you planted the seeds a little late? What if you planted the seeds and forgot about them? You are not alone. Simply begin now — where you are with the tools you have. We all stumble in this parenting thing. What do we do? We begin again. So, no matter where you are in your own faith walk, no matter what you did or didn't do with your teen in the past, begin now to invite your teen to follow you as you both explore what it means to have a mission. Use your own growth as an opportunity to lead your teen. Your teen doesn't need you to be perfect; he just needs you to step forward.

Don't Put the Mission Cart Before the Identity Horse

When our teenagers have time alone to think and pray, when they have creative outlets, ideas and dreams well up inside them as God draws them toward himself. They will likely talk to us about many of these experiences, but not all of them. We can make it safe to share without pushing or requiring it. Again, attachment and emergence co-exist in our teens. So, sometimes our teen needs us to reach down in our caretaking role, being the answer to one of his attachment needs. At other times, when those attachment needs are satiated, we will see flashes of emergence in our teens — moments of curiosity about a new hobby, about possible careers and vocations, about their mission in the Church, about what it means to be a child of God. These are questions of identity.

Society's understanding of identity has become so obscured in recent decades that it's no wonder parents struggle to help their teens through the roller coaster of emergence. If we follow the status quo, we'll walk into a minefield of conflicting and distorted messages about how teenagers figure out their identities. We do have this drive to become separate persons, but we also have a nature that is inclined to sin. Some people think that if they have the urge to do something, they need to do it in order to "be themselves." The drive to individuate can become warped. Our human drives have a natural purpose, but because of original sin, we can try to satisfy our drives in sinful, harmful ways contrary to our dignity as children of God. Because our culture shapes our identities, if the culture is sick, our perceptions of ourselves can become swept up into this sickness in one way or another. For example, in his insightful book, *Who Am I, Lord?*, Joe Heschmeyer explains that our society assumes out of the starting gate that identity is somehow about gender experiments or tribalistic identity politics. If our teen starts here, he'll become even more confused about who he is and where he needs to go because, in reality, his identity has nothing to do with those things. Our society also gets identity wrong by putting too much emphasis on performance, job status, and other external signs of success.

As Heschmeyer points out, specific questions pervade human life: *Who am I? Where have I come from? Where am I going?* These are the fundamental questions beneath all the different questions our teens ask themselves and will continue to ask themselves for the rest of their lives if they live vibrantly. Only our teens can do the work of answering those questions, but they desperately need us to help them frame these questions in a more nuanced way than society does. How our kids answer these questions will set the course for their lives and drive their actions and choices.

Teens wonder what they should do with their lives, but they can't know what they should do (their mission) unless they know who they are (their identity). Heschmeyer's point is that we can't know who we are apart from God, our Creator. Pope St. John Paul II writes in *Fides et Ratio* that "God has placed in the human heart a desire to know the truth — in a word, to know himself — so that, by knowing and loving God, men and women may also come to the fullness of truth about themselves."[2] So, when our teens ask, "Who am I?" they will find the most accurate answer by figuring out who God is. They are made in the image of God, so when they look into God's face, they see themselves. The clearer God's face becomes to our teens, the better they see the whole truth about themselves. Christ asks our teens, "Who do you say that I am?" not because he doesn't know the answer, but because our teens need to pursue the answer. Their answer to that question will open a door or close it.

Our identity is a given. We don't "invent" ourselves. We do need to do the lifelong work of understanding our identity, and this work begins in relationship with our Maker. So, if we want our teenagers to have a healthy identity grounded in truth, we must encourage and facilitate their growing relationship with God. If your teen is open to reading about what it means to have a relationship with God, check out *The Adventure: Living Out Your Relationship with God (Catholic Edition)* by Chris Patterson. For teen-friendly books on identity, I recommend *Made for More* by Curtis Martin and *I Am ___: Rewrite Your Name — Reroute Your Life* by Chris Stefanick.

Your Teen's Gifts and Passions

Sometimes our teens focus on what they are not — on their limitations or failings. They compare themselves to others or to what the popular culture expects them to be. They don't feel pretty enough, fast enough, or smart enough. God doesn't care about all that. When God looks at our kids, he sees more in them than they can possibly see. He sees more in them than even we see. He sees all their potential, their gifts, and what they can be in heaven. We see the acorn; God sees the oak. Sometimes our teens don't see any of it because they're looking in the wrong place. They look at their peers or social media influencers and imagine they are supposed to be like them. This is why healthy attachment is critical. Attachment provides a child with a mirror so he can see the truth about himself. His parents and his Creator are meant to be his mirror of attachment during emergence.

Each of our teens has unique gifts that allow them to fulfill their purpose in the world, according to God's plan. Figuring out their gifts and how to best use them is not a destination but a process that will continue for their entire lives. Whatever our teens' special gifts and talents are, they're called to use them for the good of others. This work begins in their relationships at home, then extends out to the world. If they're looking for somebody to model their lives after as they use those gifts, Christ is the standard of perfection they should follow, not their peers or social media stars.

Spend some time chatting with your teen about his passions and talents. If he has clear talents, in what contexts does he feel a sense of joy when using these talents? What is most life-giving for him? One tip to share with your teen: A natural talent isn't necessarily identical to his calling, because not every talent is life-giving or part of his mission. For example, if your teen is a great guitar player, it doesn't necessarily mean he's called to be a music minister. Maybe he'll be a philosophy teacher who happens to enjoy playing the guitar. God may use the guitar playing as an instrument to lead the teen where he needs to go, but the destination may surprise us.

I'll share an example from my family. My adult son, Aidan, is quite introverted and cerebral. He thought as a young teen that he wanted to become a military pilot. He was always interested in aviation, and he excelled in any kind of STEM class in high school. So, given his personality, passions, and academic abilities, we assumed he would become an aeronautical engineer, a pilot, or both. But when he was fifteen or so, he began doing service work regularly with our parish. He said a light came on for him; he felt most himself during those service projects. He began thinking more seriously about religious life as a result. These experiences were life-giving and a clue to how he was called to serve in the Church. These moments when our teens realize that something seems "right," when they receive spiritual graces while using their talents, help them discern which way to go, little by little, step by step. Aidan continues to be fascinated by aeronautics, and it's possible that this interest will intersect in some way with his larger mission, but he is fairly confident that he is not called to be a pilot. He believes he is called to be a priest. If he's right, then he'll be a priest who happens to like airplanes and airports! (He's the only person I know who tries to book flight itineraries with *more* airport connections!)

Your teen's interests and talents are relevant and important in discerning his call, but sometimes these things are clues to something else that God wants our teens to look at. Aidan was drawn to the virtue of self-sacrifice and radical surrender in military service; he recognized these same life-giving qualities in his volunteer work in our youth group, and he continues to experience them as he studies as a seminarian. Whatever your teen's "big" vocation may be (marriage, religious life, priesthood, etc.), he'll figure it out by living a holy life, seeking God's will, and busying himself with the tasks God asks him to do each day. God reveals our vocation gradually as we cooperate with him, learn more about ourselves, and deepen our prayer life and relationship with God. We want to make the notion of vocation part of everyday family conversation, but we don't want our teens to become obsessed with figuring it out. Another insight you might share with your teen: How our calling in the Church plays out will change depending on our primary relationships and responsibilities at different points in our lives. Since I was a young girl, I've been passionate about writing. I enjoy just about every type of writing, and I always wanted to be a professional writer. For many years, I was engaged in some kind of serious writing, whether creative, expository, or legal. However, when I was a new mother, my writing seemed limited chiefly to making grocery lists! My responsibilities and relationships limited the time I could commit to my writing, but eventually, as my children matured, God called on me to use this passion to bless others. I not only write more now, but I teach writing to many children.

Similarly, our teens' primary responsibilities today are different from what they will be in ten years; their relationships will be different depending on their state in life (marriage, religious life, single life). Right now, their primary relationships are in their families, so they should focus on fulfilling their roles and responsibilities as a sibling, son or daughter, student, and whatever other relationships they have. So, focus on helping your teen identify and explore his passions, deepen his relationship with God, and be attentive to the responsibilities and tasks required of him each day without worrying too much about what he'll be doing in ten years. Remind your teen gently that he doesn't have to figure out his entire life now; God reveals his will gradually, in small steps. While it's helpful to plan ahead and think about future vocations, he doesn't need to know everything right now. His future will become clear if he is faithful and obedient; God will reveal what your teen needs to know when he needs to know it and when he's ready to see it.

As an aside, when my son began discerning a call to the priesthood, I was rather surprised at the reactions of a few Catholic parents who said they wouldn't want their sons to become priests or their daughters to become religious sisters or nuns. The primary concern was the loss of grandchildren in their lives; the secondary concern was surrendering the children to another authority, to poverty, to cloistered life. Many parents recognize the need for more priests and religious and pray fervently that young men and women will enter these vocations, but they hope their own kids aren't called! In reality, if our children are called to religious life and they ignore the call, they will always feel that something is missing. So we love our children by encouraging them to whatever life God has planned for them; we reveal our lack of faith in God when we believe our plans for our kids are better than God's. God helps us bloom where we're planted, so I'm not suggesting such a child would be lost or miserable if they missed a religious call, but our children will more easily thrive if they heed God's plan for them. We should consider it a grave injustice to prevent our children from exploring potential religious vocations.

Raising Mission-Minded Teens in a Me-Obsessed World

While our teens ultimately must choose to pursue answers to their big questions about their identity and purpose, and while they alone must choose to be disciples of Christ, we must make mission-mindedness part of our family cultures. A concern for others is an essential aspect of Church social teaching that applies to everyone (more on this below); it's also one of the four critical tasks of the Catholic family, as outlined in Pope John Paul II's apostolic exhortation *Familiaris Consortio*. "Thus, far from being closed in on itself, the family is by nature and vocation open to other families and to society, and undertakes its social role."[3] Focusing on charitable work helps our teens exercise their empathy muscles, but it's also part of fulfilling our family's purpose as the domestic church.

Volunteering as a family can take many different forms. Sometimes opportunities come up spontaneously in the course of an average day. Maybe an elderly neighbor needs help carrying her groceries, or a tree limb falls and blocks the road. Our family can dive in to help. We can also find causes that we all care about and make it part of our family's routine to get involved. Consider your family's gifts (talents, experience) and limitations (ages of kids, schedules). Brainstorm ideas for how you can serve together on a project.

The spiritual and corporal works of mercy might be a good place to start your brainstorming. The works of mercy are ancient charitable practices found in the teachings of Jesus. They provide a model for how we can treat others, particularly when they are suffering in some way. In this way, we become Christ's witnesses. The corporal works of mercy respond to the basic bodily needs of our neighbors, while the spiritual works of mercy focus on ministering to their spiritual needs. **The corporal works of mercy** are feeding the hungry, giving drink to the thirsty, clothing the naked, sheltering the homeless, visiting the sick, visiting the prisoner, and burying the dead. **The spiritual works of mercy** are converting the sinner, instructing the ignorant, counseling the doubtful, comforting the sorrowful, bearing wrongs patiently, forgiving injuries, and praying for the living and the dead. Children learn about the works of mercy first within their family relationships. From a place of rest and safety in their relationships with us, our children learn to express love, concern, and care for their families (siblings, grandparents, cousins, etc.). They practice sharing their gifts and talents at home, and they become attuned to the joys of solidarity and mutuality in healthy communities. From there, we can accompany our teens as they bring their gifts and the love of Christ to others beyond our front doors.

Here are some ideas to get you started. Some activities will be most appropriate for parents and their older kids and teens, but there are plenty of options that can include the whole family:

- *Donate your talents*: Whatever your family's talents (art, music, technology, joke-telling, storytelling) — use them to bless others. You might visit patients in a nursing facility, create gifts for impoverished children, or donate your creative product to charity. In all these ways, you comfort the sick or the sorrowful and teach your children that we can use all our talents to glorify God.

- *Raise money for the needy*: You can also use your talents to raise money to donate to charity. My kids and their friends made homemade items, sold them, and then donated the money to an orphanage in Africa. Having a specific charity in mind helped them persevere when they hit obstacles, and it motivated patrons to buy the kids' products.
- *Volunteer at soup kitchens and food banks:* Some soup kitchens and food banks will allow families to work together. At a minimum, you can collect food and help stock shelves at a food bank, but your local food bank might have even more ways your whole family can serve together.
- *Volunteer in your parish:* Get your teen to help you teach a catechism class or lead an activity in children's ministry at your parish.
- *Help the homeless:* Assemble and deliver care packages for the homeless. One year, a few of my children and I created bundles that included mittens, toiletries, and snacks. You can also volunteer for organizations like Habitat for Humanity that revitalize or build homes for the poor and vulnerable.
- *Teach somebody to read:* Your older kids and teens can volunteer with you at a literacy or children's reading program.

Your family is the domestic church, a unique ministry in itself, a vital conduit of God's love, grace, and healing to the world.[4] This can seem intimidating, but we are not meant to do it alone. Just start somewhere, and opportunities and ideas will flow. We need only say "yes," and God will provide the path and the means for us to serve.

If your family senses a calling to take your service work a

step further, you might consider a family mission trip. The Family Missions Company is a Catholic organization that facilitates service opportunities for families in the United States and internationally. Families work together serving the poor and needy in places like Louisiana, Peru, and Taiwan.

A cautionary note about organized teen mission trips: For reasons social scientists don't completely understand yet, going on group mission trips with their peers doesn't do much for teen faith. These trips do not seem to deepen teens' spiritual lives or even increase their empathy, even when they serve in devastated mission locations. In fact, Catholic professor of sociology Christian Smith found a negative relationship between teen mission trips and retained faith.[5] Director of the Fuller Youth Institute, Kara Powell, concluded the same in her "sticky faith" research, noting that mission trips don't seem to curb American teens' materialism or increase their generosity toward the poor.[6]

Rather than sending teens on peer-centered mission trips, Powell encourages parents and caring adults to take the lead in walking alongside teenagers before, during, and after mission experiences. The mission trip should be a process of understanding and reflection, not an event to attend. We can prepare teens by previewing what they will see and experience on the mission. During the trip, we can help them reflect on what they are doing and why it matters. After the trip, we can help our teens identify how they want to change because of what they witnessed. Our teens can take the lessons they learned on the trip into their everyday lives back home. This approach turns a mission trip into a process of transformation rather than a school trip.

What impact does *family* service have on our children's faith lives? Diana Garland's research convinced her that family-centered service, whether in a soup kitchen for an afternoon or in a remote village for a week, is the gold standard when it comes to faith transmission. In her fascinating book, *Inside Out Families*, Garland explores the fruits of family service, including improved familial relationships, a renewed appreciation for family time, and the development of resilient faith in children.

When Your Teen Doesn't Want to Serve with You

What should you do if you're convinced of the importance of increasing your family's service in your community, but your teenager flatly rejects the idea? Teenagers may resist participating in service projects for many reasons. Sometimes they are anxious about novel experiences — they don't know what to expect or what will be expected of them. They think it might be weird or uncomfortable. Encourage your teen to move outside her comfort zone. While we can empathize with our teens' concerns and listen to their reasons for not wanting to volunteer, we should make family service obligatory, like helping with the dishes or visiting Grandma. Everyone participates because this is who we are as a family. This is a general principle, but you as mom or dad should use prudence in determining how to live out this principle when you're facing resistance. Lead with warmth and understanding; back off for a few weeks if you think it's prudent but return to the idea eventually.

Your teenagers will probably end up getting more out of family service than they expected. (I can't count how many times my teens thought they'd hate something and ended up liking it.) Gently remind your teen that you are serving as a family not because it's fun or entertaining but because other people need the help. Many teens learn about social issues and challenges at school and on social media. Reading about or watching videos gives kids useful information, but it doesn't change their hearts or open their eyes. Immersion in service alongside caring adults helps teens move beyond head knowledge and the idealized sound bites they hear on social media, which rarely reveal the day-to-day challenges faced by volunteers and those they serve.

My daughter Claire would watch videos about abandoned dogs, but there was no substitute for her volunteer work at an animal shelter. She eventually became a foster contact for abandoned kittens and dogs that needed a home until they were ready for adoption. This raises another important point: You don't have to dive into the deep end of a service opportunity with your teenager, especially when he or she is resistant. Take it a step at a time. Claire didn't start by fostering animals. First, she learned the ropes at the shelter for a few hours a week, doing the dirty work (literally). She had some fun and a few heartbreaks; she gained a greater appreciation for the work the adoption center was doing. After that, becoming a foster contact seemed a natural step for her.

Getting your teen's opinion on the service project options may also help her feel more comfortable and enthusiastic about contributing. Invite your teen to help you choose from possible service opportunities. Perhaps you can find out what your teen already cares about and then find service opportunities that are a good fit.

The Empathy Drought

Helping our teens develop a sense of concern for others helps counter one of the most confounding problems in Western society: Empathy is decreasing and meanness is increasing in young people. In one notable study, analysts measured empathy in new college students every year for three decades.[7] During those thirty years, empathy scores decreased by nearly 50 percent in this demographic despite an intensified focus on "niceness" in the broader society. The students admitted they care primarily about themselves and give little thought to the needs of others; in fact, they perceive this trait as an asset. Analysts believe this crisis has something to do with the rise of smartphones and social media, which permit excessive virtual connection without real human connection. As already mentioned, these are counterfeit forms of intimacy.

In response to this empathy drought, schools have implemented empathy curricula, and many experts advise parents to offer their kids rewards for nice behavior. It seems these experts have confidence that we can insert empathy into children if we give them the right ideas or attractive enough incentives. One author even suggests we can inject oxytocin molecules into people to make them more empathetic.[8] Maybe school nurses will start handing out empathy vitamins at lunch. Aside from the fact that "niceness" is overrated (sometimes doing what is best for somebody doesn't feel "nice" to them), such school and parenting programs overlook an essential truth about human nature: You cannot teach somebody to care. You can teach them to act like they care, but this is not the same as empathy.

The definition of empathy is caring coupled with consideration.[9] Empathy is a feeling of *caring* (Catholics would use the term love or charity) for somebody in response to our *consideration* of their circumstances and feelings. People can behave empathetically without really giving a hoot about anyone. Bullies have insight into the emotions of others, but they respond with dominance rather than caring. Sociopaths are adept at reading the needs and emotions of their victims, but they use their insight to exploit or manipulate them. In both the bully and the sociopath, we see consideration without caring. These people are very capable of reading others around them, but they don't respond with love. Other people have caring feelings, but they lack consideration (the ability to perspective take). In fact, this is typical and natural in toddlers and preschoolers. Because the part of the brain responsible for perspective-taking remains immature until children reach school age, they might possess intense feelings of caring but say jarring things like, "Grandpa, your belly is too big for your shirt." Small children are capable of caring, but they struggle to imagine or account for what somebody else is thinking or feeling. By the teen years, however, our kids are fully capable of taking into account the feelings of others before they act.

So, should we only require our teenagers to behave empathically when they feel caring emotions? Of course not. In principle, there's nothing wrong with character development programs, service projects, and other experiences that help children recognize compassionate actions and offer them opportunities to practice compassion in real life. What is missing in some empathy programs is the element of hierarchical relationship, which is where a child's capacity to care is actually nurtured. If we want to reduce coldness and bullying and increase empathy in the next generation, we need to reverse technology addiction and increase nurturing, hierarchical care in our children's lives. We also need to reduce messages that our love for our teens is dependent on their behavior. Caring begets caring. We want our teens to behave with virtue, and we want to have high expectations, but we don't want to withdraw (or threaten to withdraw) our love and acceptance when our children fall short. When we do, they will harden up to protect themselves, or they will do the right thing out of fear, not virtue. We should require our teenagers to do the right thing even if their hearts are not in it, but we should be aware that caring actions and caring feelings are two different kettles of fish. We want our children to behave kindly no matter their feelings, but we hope that our children come to possess truly charitable hearts and an ability to consider the needs and feelings of others.

So often, the human heart is a muddle. Sometimes we do the right thing mostly for the right reasons, but some selfish motivations may be in the mix. Fortunately, God in his goodness can work with our mixed motivations. I think if we love our teenagers generously, guide them in recognizing the virtues, offer them chances to practice the virtues, and point them to the source of virtue, God's grace is enough to sort out loose ends.

Catholic Social Teaching for Justice-Minded Teens

As an expression of their desire to better the world, some teenagers become interested in political activism. Unfortunately, teenagers can be swayed by postmodern concepts of justice, which seem appealing on the surface but often call for the dismantling and destruction of society rather than restoring people to dignity and peace. On a more subtle level, secular justice warriors often ask us to accept and even support behavior that is disordered and corrupt, all in the name of love. We can guide our teenagers toward understanding the fuller picture of what social justice entails and requires.

The 7 Principles of Catholic Social Teaching

1. Respect the human person.
2. Encourage a family-centered society.
3. Know your rights and corresponding responsibilities.
4. Lift up the poor.
5. Respect work and protect workers.
6. Work for the common good of everyone, not just yourself.
7. Care for God's creation.

God has entrusted the Church with articulating for the laity the meaning of justice within the economy of salvation. Here is a critical insight: We can never comprehend justice without first comprehending what it means to be human. The Church's teaching on social issues is complex and layered. For the sake of clarity, we usually group them into seven different categories that we call "the seven principles of Catholic social teaching." Teens may not need to know the details of all these principles, but it's helpful for parents to understand them so we can explain the Church's teachings to our kids in a coherent way. Here's a snapshot[10]:

1. Dignity of Life and the Human Person

A person's value and dignity come from the fact that he or she is made in the image and likeness of God. All human life is sacred and possesses inherent dignity. Each person enjoys this dignity regardless of how useful they are or how much money, power, or popularity they possess; regardless of their sex or race; regardless of their stage of development, from conception to death. The other principles often take as a starting point this principle about the inherent dignity of human life.

2. Call to Family, Community, and Participation

Human beings are innately social: God created us with a desire and need for companionship and community. Just as we're called to protect the dignity of each individual person, we are called to protect the dignity of social groups comprised of individuals. The family is the first and most important social group because our preparation to take our place in society begins in a family. For this reason, the *Catechism* calls the family the "original cell of social life" (2207). This principle also teaches that people in a community have a right to participate in the common good, especially in matters directly impacting them. The common good is "the sum total of social conditions" that allow people, not only as individuals but also groups, to reach their fulfillment more fully and easily.[11] When everybody has a chance to participate in improving society, we're all better off for it.

3. Rights and Responsibilities

The Church affirms that all human beings have a right to live with dignity, but they also have corresponding duties in society. We have a right to life, but we also have a responsibility to care for ourselves. We have a right to make a living wage to support our families, but we also have a responsibility to live within our means. We have a right to search for truth and live out our faith, but we also have a responsibility to live in the truth that we find. A society is more just when we strike a balance between these rights and duties. We hear many in our society demanding their rights, but they are less concerned about their duties or about violating the rights of others. This is a subtle but important insight to share with our teenagers. Ironically, if we demand our own rights while ignoring the duties connected to these rights, none of us can live with dignity.

4. Option for the Poor and Vulnerable

This principle reminds us to prioritize the needs of the impoverished and vulnerable when making decisions. We do what we can to lift them out of their situations and facilitate their growth. From her beginning, the Church has demonstrated a special concern for the poor, homeless, and forgotten. Poverty has to do with a lack of material needs but also poverty of soul (psychological suffering) and poverty of addiction (including a disordered desire for objects, beauty, sex, or admiration). Our families can work together to alleviate poverty by practicing the spiritual and corporal works of mercy, as suggested above.

5. The Dignity of Work and Rights of Workers

Work is dignified because, through our work, we participate in God's creative activity in the world. Work reflects God in us. We have a right and a duty to work, and we have a right to fair working conditions. The Church's efforts in defense of workers' rights have been influential globally. Many of the rights we take for granted were first advanced by the Church, including the rights to a just wage, safe working conditions, and time for rest.[12] God's plan is not that we barely survive; we have a right to work for a better life for ourselves and our families.

6. *Solidarity*

According to the Church, despite our tendency to look out for number one, we *are* our brothers' and sisters' keepers (see Gn 4:9). We are not solitary beings disconnected from other people and communities. Our choices impact others, often in ways we don't appreciate. Solidarity is a principle highlighting this inter-connection and interdependence. John Paul II emphasized that solidarity is more a virtue than a feeling: "On the contrary, it is a firm and persevering determination to commit oneself to the common good; that is to say to the good of all and of each in-dividual, because we are all really responsible for all."[13] We are called to offer ourselves for the good of our neighbor, with a readiness to serve rather than use him.

7. *Caring for God's Creation*

Your teen may be surprised to learn that the Church is pro-en-vironment! As stewards of the created world, we can show our respect for and gratitude to God by our care for the Earth. We shouldn't use the natural world in any way we want just because it serves us. We must consider "the nature of each being and its mutual connection in an ordered system, which is precisely the cosmos."[14] The Church's work on environmental justice origi-nates in its commitment to protecting the dignity of all human-ity. We can't understand environmental and ecological issues apart from human experience and communities.

These seven principles are not about economic theories or political policies but about forming the consciences of the faithful. Catholics of goodwill can disagree about how we might achieve the goals outlined in the principles.[15] They're common-sense ideas about how we should treat each other. They apply to every person, not just Catholics. While these ideals are challenging, our families can work toward their realization by allowing them to guide our choices a little more each day.

Reflection and Direction

- Our work as missionary families begins at home. Study the corporal and spiritual works of mercy with your kids, then look for practical ways to serve each other at home.
- Help your teen identify ways to practice the works of mercy with his family. For example, when your teen helps feed his baby sister, point out that he's feeding the hungry!
- After your family has home-based mission work down, find ways to serve together in your parish or community. You can connect these to seasonal traditions. For example, during Lent, do a 40-day clear out of your closets to put together donations for charity shops.

4
Forging a Faith Village for Your Teen

If a blind man leads a blind man, both will fall into a pit.
— Matthew 15:14

The Big Picture
- Adding adults to your teen's attachment village
- Why youth groups aren't building teen faith
- Tips for implementing a multi-generational faith program at your parish

In the last chapter, I mentioned that social scientists identify new technologies as contributing to the problem of declining empathy in young people. An additional explanation for this decrease in empathy is the increase in peer orientation in children and teens.[1] Once again, peer orientation is the Trojan horse that nobody pays attention to because we assume it's a natural part of the landscape. We facilitate premature socializing in our young children, and we believe our teens' addiction to peer contact is normal and natural (it's the norm, but it's unnatural). So, our children retreat from attachments to us when we are meant to keep them safe and help them grow up.

I touched on these issues in previous chapters, but here is a snapshot of what our children lose when they withdraw from healthy hierarchical attachment relationships:

- They lose their shield against peer wounding. (Parents and other adults provide a shield that renders mostly inert the mean things peers might do or say).
- They lose their intuition to adopt our language, values, and culture. (Peer orientation may be one reason adolescent vocabulary has contracted in the last fifty years.)
- They fail to develop resilience against disappointment. (Parents and other adults provide children and teens with a safe outlet for the frustration they experience from setbacks and losses so they can ultimately bounce back and grow through them.)
- They lose emotional rest and true play. (When children feel safe in healthy hierarchical relation-

ships, they can come to emotional rest. Only when
our children are at emotional rest are they free to
explore and play, particularly in solitude. This is as
true for teens as it is for small kids.)

- They lose their caring feelings. (To care too much
is threatening for peer-oriented children.)

All of these losses add up. The more a teen cares about mattering to her peers, the less she can afford to care about anybody.
Why? Because teenagers know it's emotionally dangerous to
depend on their peers to meet their emotional needs, so they
become defended against "soft" emotions. Peer-oriented kids
are fiercely competitive and jealous, and some of them become
bullies or victims of bullying. They can be insensitive and even
cruel and narcissistic. Or the teen may pursue her peers' acceptance and admiration so intensely that she loses sight of her inherent dignity and unique gifts; she may judge herself through
her peers' eyes, which rarely see the whole picture.

Recall the attachment yearning to belong. Throughout human history, parents have intuited that children belong with
the adults who are responsible for their well-being. We have
lost our way as a society. We assume our children belong with
other children because they're the same size and at the same
developmental stage. We need our kids to know they belong
with us so we can lead them to their emotional, intellectual,
social, and spiritual potential. This is especially true for teens.
When our teens know they belong with us, they won't feel
threatened when they notice the many ways they are different
from their peers. Their sense of belonging with us gives them
a way to hold on to us even when their developmental destiny
somehow separates them from their peers (or, indeed, even us).

Recall, too, the attachment yearning to be significant, to
matter. When our teens know they matter to us, it frees them to

grow up; when they need to matter to their peers, they become enslaved. Peer-oriented kids are incredibly insecure because peers are so fickle. No matter how popular they are, they know intuitively that their popularity — their mattering — is easily cancelable if they break one of those elusive, capricious rules that makes you a teen "insider." They know their significance is fragile. They can go from popular to unpopular because they get a haircut.

If we aren't the answer to our kids' attachment needs, they can also depersonalize attachment: They take humans out of the attachment equation altogether. They try to fill the attachment void by winning games and placing academically; they become addicted to social media, pornography, or casual sex; they become obsessed with their appearance. (Note, this kind of depersonalized attachment is prevalent in adults with an avoidant attachment status.)

Recognize the Trojan horse and reclaim your children. Our kids need us to take the lead and draw them back into natural hierarchical care. When our kids hit the teen years, this care includes other grown-ups besides ourselves. We can provide our teenagers with a village of care in which adults shower them with love and support.

I want to share some tips for building an attachment village for teenagers, particularly a faith village. Let me begin by explaining how we can create a network of adults who take an interest in our teens and who are willing to mentor, redirect, and celebrate them. Then we'll take a look at our parishes: Why aren't our teen youth programs working, and what can parents do about it?

Matching Your Teen to Grown-Ups

Protecting the relationship between ourselves and our teens is difficult when the social norm invites distance and even fracturing in the parent-teen relationship. We really do have to be countercultural. Frankly, we have to be willing to be the weird parents.

First, we need to be aware of our teens' exposure to unsupervised peer interactions, including social media use and peer group gatherings. If such exposure is excessive or creates attachment issues, we need to reduce it. We want to welcome our teens' friends into our homes, but we should ensure we remain a benevolent presence. Look at your teen's calendar and the dynamics in the groups in which he participates. If he's involved in many peer-dominated groups, try to replace a few with activities led by caring adults. For example, if he's involved in a school club run by the kids without adult leadership, balance this with another activity led by a wise and engaged adult.

Second, instead of peers, our teens need more adults around who care about them. Match your teen to trusted friends, family members, and other adults who care about your teen: grandparents, aunts, uncles, coaches, godparents, to name a few.[2] How can you facilitate these relationships? Often, you don't need to say anything because the adult has a strong lead already in the relationship with your teen. But, if necessary, talk to these adults about how important they are in your teen's life and ask them if they'd be willing to spend some time with your teen regularly. Create rituals and traditions that connect teens to these adults; use the attachment roots of sameness, belonging, and significance to forge a stronger connection between them. For example, mention to Grandpa how much your teen loves fishing with him, and mention to your teen the compliment Grandpa shared about his fly-fishing skills. We want to encourage these adults to take a strong attachment stance with our kids, and we want our kids to feel at home emotionally with these adults.

Ensuring Safety

Unfortunately, we live in a time when we must be alert to potential adult exploitation of our children and teens. Here are some common tactics groomers use to lure in victims. Discuss these behaviors with your teen, and let her know she can come to you if she feels uncomfortable with an adult.

1. Selecting: Predators select targets who are vulnerable in some way, especially kids with troubled home relationships, so one of the best ways to protect teens from adult predators is to protect the parent-teen relationship. Predators manipulate a teen's feelings of inadequacy and isolation for their own purposes. They make the teen feel that they're the only one who understands them or cares about them. No adult mentoring your teen should create division in your relationship — if an adult says things that alienate your teen from you, immediately sever the contact and alert relevant leadership to the problem.

2. Gaining Trust: Groomers often try to gain a teen's trust through flattery and gifts. They make the teen feel "special." It's fine for a grandparent or friend to give your teens gifts and compliments, but if an adult offers your teen secret gifts or odd compliments ("You have the prettiest hair of any of the girls"), she should immediately inform a parent or other adult leader.

3. Isolation: Groomers figure out what victims like and use it to manipulate the teen into isolated scenarios. For example, they get the teen's favorite music or games and invite them to join them. Again, it's fine for grown-ups to play with teens! It's a great way to build rapport. But explain to your teen that

an adult should never draw them away from groups or invite them to play alone without another adult's presence or knowledge.

4. Gradual Touching: Groomers may begin touching victims innocuously, getting them comfortable with the groomer's touching. Then they use the trust they've built to go further. Ensure your teen knows that no adult should touch them anywhere other than their shoulder or hand. Brief hugs are okay, but the adult's lower body should not touch the teen's body. Many safe environment trainers recommend that adult leaders only hug students from the side around the shoulder — so a little shoulder squeeze while both people are facing forward in the same direction.

Teens will tend to follow adults who make them feel relaxed and welcomed. My eleventh-grade literature teacher, Miss Fahrion, took a particular interest in me when I joined her class partway through the school year. I had moved from out of state and didn't know anybody in the school. It was a time of rupture and uncertainty in my life. When I expressed an interest in Shakespeare, she took the time to chat with me about literature and writing. She loaned me books from her private library. She found a way to reach me through a shared interest. I remember her to this day, and I'm confident that her caring attention stoked my enduring affection for literature. Many teenagers need adults like Miss Fahrion who invite connection without overwhelming attention.

We can also arrange social gatherings where adults are visibly in charge; for example, multi-family picnics, baseball games, or camping trips. Social arrangements where whole families gather together are healthier for the children than peer gatherings.[3] For example, instead of a junior high dance with dozens of twelve-year-olds crammed together in a gym with a handful of adults talking in a corner, have a family dance where every child has a parent present, mingling with other parents and children. In these gatherings, the children know the adults are there to protect them; the children are there to have fun, not to get their emotional needs met. In intuitive cultures, families to this day gather in this way; the kids play under the protective gaze of many generations of adults. As a result, the kids grow up with a greater sense of rootedness and connection to an adult-oriented world where they naturally follow the lead of grown-ups and absorb the values and culture of the previous generation.

Finally, ensure your teen's teachers and coaches know how much they mean to your teen.[4] Ideally, parents would have the freedom to carefully choose the substitute attachment figures in their children's lives, but nowadays, we often have no choice about who is in charge of our children in particular settings. We either accept the soccer coach, or our child doesn't play soccer. So, we have to facilitate the connection sometimes. Adults who take formal leadership roles in children's lives tend to care deeply about kids, but sometimes they doubt they're making a difference, or they assume parents don't want adults to be too friendly with their children. So we have to tell them and show them, and in doing so, we are tapping into their natural attachment instincts. As a teacher, I can tell you that adults who teach and lead children appreciate it when parents mention specific ways the adults have impacted their children. Prime the attachment pump with simple gestures and words of encouragement. My daughter mentioned to me several times how much her art teacher has changed her life and helped her artistic skills. I passed this on to the art teacher, thanking her for sharing her gifts with my daughter. I then shared with my daughter the kind words the teacher used to describe my daughter's character and artistic skills. I took the lead in matching the art teacher to my daughter so the teacher would be more inclined to take my daughter under her wing, particularly with her art.

Forming Your Teen's Faith Village

Hierarchical villages also bolster teens' faith lives. In a previous chapter, I talked about how much our teens need to feel valued by their faith communities during the affiliative faith stage. The affiliative faith stage (which our kids may enter as early as the tween years) is marked by an increasing desire to make a difference in a faith community. They need to know they matter to the community — not just to the kids but also the adults. Ideally, the adults in our parishes (laity, leaders, clergy) should take an interest in our young people. In one of their surveys, Kara Powell's sticky faith research team wanted to figure out which church activities were correlated with strong faith in older teens and young adults. (For this particular study, they were looking at church-based activities, not family-based or private faith activities.) They found the most helpful activity was multi-family faith groups where whole families receive faith formation together.[5] Powell asserts that every teenager needs a minimum of five faith-building adults in their lives, in addition to coaches, teachers, and other adults who support their growth in other ways.

Because this is a book about evangelizing teens, I think it's critical for parents to know what they are up against when it comes to parish-based teen faith groups. You simply can't depend on your parish youth program to effectively shape your teen's faith life. Everyone involved in teen catechesis knows that the typical format we use to deliver youth ministry has failed miserably at forming life-long disciples. Parish youth leaders do everything they can to entice young people through the door. They use flashy programs, games, and silly skits, believing that the kids will love the group and become well-formed disciples.

In fact, one study asked teens what they wanted most in their youth groups. Games came in dead last in the list of thirteen activities; the first was meaningful conversations.[6] Most parish youth programs emphasize size. They assume the size of the program is a sign of its success; that if the youth group is big, the faith lives of the kids will be big. There is no correlation between the size of a youth program and the successful transmission of enduring faith to teenagers. Indeed, some of the most effective youth programs are small.

In his intriguing and important book, Everett Fritz points out problems in Catholic youth ministry that echo Dr. Neufeld's concerns about peer orientation in adolescent sub-culture. Regardless of the programs or materials they use, Fritz says parishes too often miss the most important thing teens need in their faith journeys: relationships with adults. "A youth group tries to create an entertaining or interactive presentation of the Faith for a large number of teenagers in one space. Yet successful youth ministry has little to do with the programs presented to teens and everything to do with the relationships that teens have with the people mentoring them."[7] Fritz argues that we should let go of the youth *group* mentality altogether and instead focus on youth *ministry*. I had always used the terms "youth group" and "youth ministry" interchangeably, but Fritz is right to distinguish them. When we minister to somebody, we meet their basic pastoral needs — needs that often cannot be met in a group setting.

Teens' basic pastoral needs have little to do with some of the things we spend our time doing in our parish youth programs. As we've learned in earlier chapters, all human beings have basic yearnings to be invited to draw close, to matter, to belong, to be understood, and to be loved deeply. So many teens are thirsting to have these basic needs met. When teenagers are in a room with thirty other teenagers, most of whom are strangers to them, they feel no sense of connection, and they are right to be guarded.

So, the Trojan horse is sitting in our parishes, too. How did Christ form his disciples? By nurturing and building close relationships. He lived side-by-side with his disciples, teaching them how to see, understand, and respond to the world as he did. Jesus didn't let the disciples teach each other. He mentored his inner circle in an intimate community where he taught them how to mentor others.

We must invite teenagers into healthy, personal mentoring relationships with grown-ups rather than pushing them into big, isolated groups of peers. We must integrate teenagers into the adult world in our parishes where they can be better formed by our culture, values, traditions, and ideas. Our teens need to observe in adults who care about them the habits of discipleship like prayer, Scripture study, service, and growth in virtue.

Here are a few ideas for family-centered approaches to faith formation where many generations worship, work, and learn together.

Micro-ministry teams

One approach is to match a single adult to a small group of teens; the adult leads the teens in some area of spiritual growth or catechetical formation, depending on the adult's gifts and the teens' needs. After the adult leads these teens for a while, we match these teens to service opportunities in the parish or community where their gifts are appreciated and developed under the continued mentorship of the original adult leader and other adults. These teenagers could even become mentors to younger children in the parish, perhaps teaching these children what they've learned from their mentor and sharing some of their own gifts with the children. While we want to de-emphasize peer orientation, we should emphasize this kind of cascading care, where adults mentor and inspire our teens, and our teens in turn mentor and inspire younger children. Cascading care is very common in intuitive communities where adults take a strong lead with children. The older children tend to fawn over younger children, practicing the virtues of love and hospitality in hierarchical relationships.

We see an example of this kind of cascading care in the quiet leadership of Jan Tyranowski in his parish during World War II. Tyranowski was a poor tailor in Nazi-occupied Poland who had a rich devotional life and studied the spirituality of St. John of the Cross. After the Nazis' brutal suppression of Christianity left many parishes without priests, Tyranowski decided to take some boys under his wing to nurture their faith lives. He could have withdrawn into his own inner world and ignored the needs of the next generation, but he didn't. He couldn't allow the young people in his parish to flounder. Risking his own life, he started a clandestine group in which he gave formation and spiritual direction to a core group of boys, guiding them and nurturing their spiritual lives and habits of virtue. When Tyranowski thought they were ready, these older boys each took a group of younger boys under their wings to guide them as Tyranowski had guided them. It was called a "Living Rosary" because the original group had five boys, and each of these boys mentored twelve little boys. Five became sixty-five!

One of the boys in Tyranowski's first core group was Karol Wojtyla, who later became Pope John Paul II. Biographer George Weigl writes of the impact Tyranowski had on the future pope and his friends:

> For the young Karol Wojtyła and his friends in the first
> Living Rosary groups, Tyranowski represented a unique
> lay combination of personal holiness and apostolic zeal,
> a kind of life "that was completely unknown to us be-
> fore." What drew them to him was his ability to "shape
> souls" by showing how "religious truths" were "not in-

terdictions [or] limitations" but the means to form "a
life which through mercy becomes [a] participation
in the life of God." To do this with adolescents — with
their distinctive combination of self-assurance and self-
doubt — was no mean accomplishment. And it seems
to have been a matter of personal example as much as
formal teaching. As Karol Wojtyła later wrote, his way of
life "proved that one could not only inquire about God
but that one could live with God."[8]

Tyranowski led the boys to discipleship through the power of his
example and relentless love. He shared what he had — his spiritual insights and devotional practices. We all have gifts we can
share with young people. They need our willingness and dedica-
tion. To make it work as a parish program, we would need several adults willing to share their time with young people, which
is admittedly an obstacle, but not an impossible one. If you think
this model would work for your parish, go for it! Like the first
disciples who took a few fishes and loaves from the Lord and
worked with what they had, work with what you have. Like the
fishes and loaves overflowing the first disciples' baskets, God will
multiply what you have. You need only bring your trust and your
willingness to serve. If you only have two adults willing to serve,
match each adult with five to eight teens at most. If prudent or
required for safe environment purposes, the groups can meet in
the same room, or a parent could volunteer to assist the main
leader in each group so no adult is alone with the teens. The key
is to meet the teens' pastoral needs and inspire them in their
faith life. This is far more likely to happen in a long-term close
mentorship with a single adult and a handful of peers than in a
huge group of peers led by one or two frazzled adults.

The adults might lead the kids in Scripture study, prayer
practices, Eucharistic adoration, apologetics, vocational discern-

ment — whatever the adult has to share with the teens. If your adult mentors need no-prep resources, check out *Quick Catholic Lessons with Fr. Mike* from Ascension Press (also recommended for "No T.O.T.T. Nights" in chapter two). This guide provides lessons and prayers to accompany several of Fr. Mike Schmitz's YouTube videos, including "Why Be Catholic?," "Is It Okay to Judge Someone?," and "The Meaning of Suffering." I also recommend the resources from YDisciple. YDisciple was created by Net Ministries, and most of their materials are now available through Formed. They provide short, engaging, high-quality videos and teaching materials. I went through some of the YDisciple topics with my teenagers at home, including "Never Alone," "Who Am I?," and "Who Is God?" I find that having the topics laid out for me along with some materials to get started reduces mentorship intimidation. However, it's okay to suspend the lesson plan and discussion topics in your micro-ministry groups when conversations naturally lead in new directions.

Intergenerational faith formation
Another idea would be to form groups of whole families so that teens, their siblings, and parents receive formation together alongside other families. This is the model Kara Powell believes is the most beneficial for teen faith development. Most parishes use a classroom model for catechism: Once a week, the parent presents the child to the catechist at the door, the parent walks away, the child joins a classroom full of same-age children, and these children spend an hour learning from a textbook with the catechist. We know this model isn't working. Kids don't seem to internalize the Faith or even remember much of what they're taught, and the model takes parents out of the picture entirely. In fact, most social scientists who look at faith transmission believe the lack of parental involvement is the most critical problem in parish catechetical programs. Without parents reinforcing and building upon

parish-based catechesis, faith won't stick. Unquestionably, parents are the most powerful agents of faith formation in their children's lives. Catholic sociologist Christian Smith remarks:

> Parents exert far and away the greatest influence on their children's religious outcomes. ... The empirical evidence is clear. In almost every case, no other institution or program comes close to shaping youth religiously as their parents do — not religious congregations, youth groups, faith-based schools, missions and service trips, summer camps, Sunday school, youth ministers, or anything else. Those influences can reinforce the influence of parents, but almost never do they surpass or override it.[9]

The Church has long taught that parents are the primary educators of their children in faith and morals: "Since they have given life to their children, parents have a most grave obligation and possess the right to educate them. ... Parents above others are obliged to form their children by word and example in faith and in the practice of Christian life."[10] Most current models have not reflected this priority, so parents can advocate for approaches that flip the model to a more family-centered one. Many parish leaders would welcome parents willing to help them move toward programs that form the whole family together or form the parents who in turn form their children. This approach is typically called intergenerational faith formation.

Intergenerational faith formation has been around for a while, with mixed success. In some programs, whole families come together for catechesis, socializing, and spiritual nourishment. In other programs, the families are all together at the beginning of a formation meeting; then, children go off to receive traditional grade-level catechesis in classrooms while the parents receive training and ideas for living the Faith at home.

This "trickle down" approach is appealing, and it's a move in the right direction. In addition to bringing parents back into the picture, it provides a village of adult mentors for children of all ages. The approach also provides opportunities for teens to nurture younger kids, as in the Living Rosary model.

However, two common problems persist in the way parishes typically implement intergenerational faith formation. First, Catholic intergenerational faith programs can be rich with relationship building but anemic in content, often glossing over or diluting Church teaching. The programs focus on games, crafts, and food, which is terrific. But parents are left with the task of catechizing their children, often with minimal support. This is less of an issue if the parents are well-formed, but parents who themselves have received poor evangelization often struggle to explain basic Church teaching to their children. We simply can't sacrifice sound teaching for community building; we need both.

Second, the programs often exclude teenagers. I attended a rollout event for one Catholic publisher's "family catechesis" program. I was very excited about the concept and beautiful materials, but the program only provided ideas for family faith formation with elementary-aged children. When I asked the publisher's representative why the program didn't include ideas for bringing teenagers into the activities and conversations, he said that teenagers wouldn't be interested in participating, and they have their own teen groups already. Precisely the problem! Any *family* faith program should include the entire family.

An intergenerational faith formation program can work if it's catechetically robust and includes teenagers. This might mean we use a decent family formation program like Family of Faith from Sophia Institute for Teachers, which has materials focusing on kids in grades kindergarten through grade six, but supplement it with special topics for teens. Sophia Institute sells thematic supplements that would work well with Family of

Faith; the supplements include topics like "The Power of Prayer," "The Beatitudes," and "Human Sexuality." In fact, any of these thematic supplements could work in the micro-ministry teams described above. We could have a Living Rosary of teens along- side a pre-prepared family formation program. This way, we can also include other adults in our parishes who may not be mem- bers of the families enrolled in the parish catechetical program. The more caring adults in our teens' lives, the better!

One advantage of this approach is that a parish would no longer require so many grade-level catechists. Instead, catechists could serve in the family formation program, which would prob- ably meet only once or twice per month. If families meet twice a month, one meeting could be a teaching meeting, and the second meeting could be a liturgical celebration. Parents may need their own mini-series on Church teachings, so they gain confidence in evangelizing their children. If parents are concerned about adding another thing to their calendars, this parent formation could be delivered in a flexible format on the parents' own time through virtual programs like those found on Formed or Word on Fire.

When Your Parish Is Stuck

Preferably these ideas would be implemented with your parish leadership, but you can also take the lead and create groups like these with other families regardless of the location of your meet- ings. Indeed, the Living Rosary group met in Tyranowski's home, not the parish building. We can view "youth ministry" as part of the ministry of family. That's right: Your family life is a ministry in itself. Discipline, food preparation, laundry, family prayers, and, yes, teen ministry are part of your family ministry! Micro-minis- try teams and intergenerational faith formation are doable onsite in a parish building, in our living rooms, or even at a park. Your parish doesn't stop being a parish when you exit the doors. So, if you're convinced that teenagers need a less peer-oriented youth ministry, but your parish is not quite as convinced, don't be too discouraged. Instead, get creative. You can create micro-ministry teams or intergenerational faith groups that meet together privately in family homes. Ensure the parents understand that this is not a drop-off youth program; the adults are critical to the success of the groups. You can take turns meeting in different homes, with everyone pitching in to provide food, materials, and teaching.

You can also use your parish's youth program to launch a home-based catechesis for your teens (and their friends, if you feel called to lead them and other parents are willing to help out). So your teen could remain involved in your parish's program, but you could supplement with more formation at home, focusing on things your teen might not be getting in the parish program. Catechist Frank Mercadente suggests that adolescent faith formation involves three dimensions: the head (passing on a cognitive understanding of the Faith), the heart (a passion for Christ and his Church), and the hands (expressing faith through concrete actions).[11] The three dimensions complement one another, and a good youth ministry program will nurture growth in all three areas. "The faith of the head finds its best expression when one's heart abides in the presence of God, and one's mission reflects the love of ways of Jesus. The passion of one's heart is best channeled when embanked by sound Catholic teaching, and expressed in concrete acts of love."[12] In reality, most youth programs emphasize one dimension to the exclusion or diminishment of the other two.

With these three areas of ministry in mind, where does your parish's youth ministry program shine, and where does it fade? For example, do you see an admirable emphasis on personal encounters with Jesus but perhaps inadequate attention to service or solid theology? You can provide a home-based ministry for your teen that shores up the deficiencies in your parish's program. Check out the resources I've already mentioned: YDisciple, Formed, Family of Faith, and Fr. Mike Schmitz. In my book,

Discipleship Parenting, I provide tips for enriching your family's Catholic identity through prayer practices, devotionals, sacred art and music, and more. Take small steps. Choose a few resources, set aside time on your calendar, and just start. You don't need to know everything; you only need enthusiasm and curiosity about the Faith. Grow alongside your teen.

In this "inspire" section, we've looked at how you can inspire your teen's sense of belonging and purpose in the Church. I've focused on ways you can lead your teen toward a sense of mission as a Christian disciple, and I've highlighted the role of trusted adults in inspiring your teen as he matures spiritually, intellectually, and emotionally. Parents and other caring adults are the answer to peer orientation, hardened hearts, and faith drift. When parents understand the purpose and power of hierarchical care in healthy relationships, they become more confident in doing what is right for their teens, regardless of what their friends are doing or what schools, magazines, or social media tell them they should be doing. Oftentimes, well-meaning advice-givers (including supposed experts) merely describe what they see, assuming it's the way it's supposed to be. They see children and teens obsessing about peers, and they assume it's part of healthy development. In ideal circumstances, teenagers continue to follow their parents' lead and the modeling of adult mentors as they get their feet inside their own shoes and walk down the path God has planned for them. Our teens will only get where they need to go if they are following the right people.

Of course, our teenagers have free will. Sometimes they don't listen to us or follow us, no matter which books we've read or how well-informed we are about human development. Like us, they do things they know are wrong; they even do things they know will ultimately hurt themselves or others. In the next section, "Freed," we'll take a look at your teen's moral development and how to handle conflict with your teen.

Reflection and Direction

- Consider the adults around your teen. Who inspires your teen? A coach or teacher? Does an adult relative have a special connection with your teen? Brainstorm three ways you can encourage the attachment dance between these adults and your teen.
- Prayerfully consider where God might be calling you to lead a youth ministry project. If you feel you're unqualified — perhaps you feel too shy or unprepared — don't let these initial concerns stop you from stepping forward in faith. Think of Our Lady, who was but a teenager when she offered her *fiat*; she didn't know what to expect, but she agreed to cooperate with God's plan. God often uses the seemingly unprepared and unqualified to create needed change and provide a unique vision. Saint Paul wrote to the Corinthians, "For consider your call, brethren; not many of you were wise according to the flesh, not many were powerful, not many were of noble birth; but God chose the foolish in the world to shame the wise, God chose what is weak in the world to shame the strong, God chose what is low and despised in the world, even things that are not, to bring to nothing things that are, so that no flesh might boast in the presence of God" (1 Cor 1:26–29). Where you are weak, Christ's glory will shine.

Free

5
Mentoring Your Teen in Discernment

For I know the plans I have for you, says the Lord, plans for welfare and not for evil, to give you a future and a hope.
— JEREMIAH 29:11

The Big Picture
- Teaching teens how to discern enduring happiness
- Teaching teens how to make wise choices
- Teaching teens how to spot a great friend

Adolescence is a time of equipping our children with the wisdom they need to make sound decisions in adulthood. Our teens will face many choices that feel overwhelming or confusing to them. What makes a choice good or bad? How do they choose between two good options in life? What makes somebody a good or bad friend? We want them to come to such decision-making with an understanding of their identity as beloved children of God. Without guidance, our teenagers can remain shallow and immature well into adulthood, seeking only to satisfy their immediate impulses, lacking an understanding of the nature of real happiness and a good life. We equip them through conversations and guidance in everyday life. It's within the safety of their relationship with us that our teens can grow into prudent and discerning disciples, capable of doing the right thing for the right reasons from a secure sense of self, knowing they are loved by us and by God.

Parents: Interrupters-In-Chief

We're raising our children in a post-Christian world in which fundamental truths about God, human nature, and our purpose in the world are no longer accepted. Western civilization has been on a trajectory of moral decay for many decades. Adding to this problem, some practitioners and theorists in the social sciences assume that in order to experience happiness and avoid pathologies, people need to create and follow their own rules or values. This erroneous assumption has become so entrenched in modern consciousness that few people notice it, let alone question it. In reality, the more a person tries to live in a moral order of his own making, the more lost and depressed he becomes. Yet, this is the world our teens live in — a world where growing up means creating their own "truth" and happiness requires others to affirm it. In the face of this insanity, the Church has remained firm in upholding the existence of immutable and foundational moral principles that are revealed by God or found in the natural order. Consequently, our teens face dilemmas and conflicting messages about what constitutes a "good" action. They will notice their friends doing things and holding opinions that conflict with our Faith and values.

When they have a difficult choice to make, like most of us, our teens will tend to follow the path of least resistance. They'll follow the crowd mindlessly unless this tendency is interrupted in some way. One of our key roles as parents is to be the Interrupters-in-Chief! We need to be interrupters because our teens have a very tenuous sense of self alongside an exaggerated sense that people are paying attention to them. As a result, even well-formed, virtuous teenagers can find themselves saying and doing things they know are wrong. Of course, such failure is partly the consequence of the Fall and human frailty, but for teenagers, it's partly a survival instinct when they are around people they know they can't trust with their inner world — their big questions, budding faith, and noble ideas.

We also need to be interrupters because teenagers tend to be impulsive and poor at assessing risk. The brain's reward structure ("that felt good; let's do it again") develops rapidly during adolescence, but the prefrontal cortex, which governs self-control, doesn't develop fully until around age twenty-five. It's our duty to set limits on our teens' behavior that is damaging to them or others. We're not being controlling or mean by not letting them attend events or participate in activities that violate our values or pose temptations that they aren't mature enough to handle. As they mature, we can give them more independence and choices, but when they are too immature to manage particular circumstances, we have to limit their independence to protect them from harm.

If our teens remain rooted in safe attachment relationships with us and other adult guides, we can provide them with many tools of discernment that will help them become less inclined to follow the crowd mindlessly.

Growing Past Pleasure

To start, let's help our teens have a more elevated understanding of happiness than the broader society. Most people assume that as long as they can pursue pleasure (without restrictions or consequences), they will be happy. More specifically, they think more pleasure equals more happiness, and the most pleasure (with the least restrictions and least consequences) equals the most happiness. This outlook is unsurprising in adolescence, but we can guide our teens toward a more nuanced vision of what will lead them to the greatest and most enduring happiness.

Across the centuries, philosophers and theologians have spilled much ink about what will make us happy. They almost unanimously agree that worldly pleasures will never lead to enduring happiness. When philosophers talk about levels or grades of happiness, pleasure sits at the bottom level. Pleasure is found in things that are external to us: food, clothing, games. Pleasure often satisfies our sensorial appetites in some way. We find pleasure in eating a candy bar, but after it's gone, the pleasure is over. Sometimes we even have a stomachache afterward. We find pleasure in buying a new dress, but the novelty wears off quickly. Sure, we feel happy when we are eating the candy bar or wearing the new dress. There's nothing wrong with these things in themselves. They are part of the created world, and the created world is good. However, they are not the highest good. When we treat them like they are the highest or only good, we take a wrong turn. The happiness we experience in these pleasurable things and activities tends to be very short-lived. If we limit ourselves to seeking happiness in these things, we will live small and unsatisfying lives. We will also tend to live selfish lives, as we focus on getting our own needs met at the expense of others.

The *Catechism* explains that our desire for happiness has a divine origin: "God has placed it in the human heart in order to draw man to the One who alone can fulfill it" (1718). God alone fulfills our hunger for happiness. We're really yearning for the happiness we will experience in communion with God in heaven; our entire being thirsts for it. While enduring happiness is reserved for heaven, we can experience a taste of it in this life by dedicating ourselves to growing in holiness and deepening our love for God. The more we surrender our own plans for God's, the greater happiness we experience in this life. We become happier when we begin asking questions about our purpose, what is truly valuable, and what it means to live a good life. Sometimes we're not sure of the answers, but merely asking these questions leads to a more fulfilling life than eating candy bars and buying new dresses. Happiness comes from making a contribution to the world and by recognizing and appreciating the beauty and gifts in others. And in one of the greatest paradoxes of human existence, we become happier the more we empty ourselves for the sake of others.

Many teenagers become stuck in pursuing happiness in pleasure because of marketing, cultural conditioning, and a desire to fit in. They believe that if they have the latest new gadgets, then they'll be happy. We have to interrupt this tendency. One of my sons used to spend a little too much time dreaming about buying things — a new scooter, a new piece of technology, a new airsoft gun. He would get the new thing, use it for a while, then spend a lot of time planning his purchase of the next new thing. So, I gently pointed out to him that these things he desired weren't bad in themselves, but they couldn't make him happy for very long. The deep satisfaction he was hunting for would never be found in those objects. I also pointed out how marketing rarely matches reality; marketers use our fears and weaknesses to convince us to buy their stuff. As long as he understood these points, he would make wiser buying decisions. It's a message I will surely need to repeat, and, given I sometimes want something new for no better reason than the marketing was good, I will do so with humility and patience!

Note that there is a difference between an immature understanding of happiness and an avoidant attachment style. People struggling with avoidant attachment may attach to physical objects to replace their need for intimate human connection. So, they may hoard their belongings or become addicted to shopping.

Searching Below Surface Desires

Spiritual directors tell us that God communicates with us directly, sometimes through our desires. They are not talking about our superficial, surface desires for material objects or similar pleasures. But, if we search below these desires, God may direct our attention to something we need to see, or he may reveal a more fundamental desire being masked by the surface desire. Many times, we discover an emotional yearning below these desires. For example, on the surface, a teen might desire a new phone; below the surface she yearns for connection and belonging. A young teenager in one of my literature classes once said that his goal in life is to become very wealthy and live in a mansion. When I began asking him more about these dreams, it seemed he was really looking for security and respect; his desire for wealth was a cover for this deeper yearning.

Surface desires can be an anesthetic, preventing us from experiencing a displaced emotion. People with avoidant attachment have a chronic fear of failure or losing face; people with anxious attachment often have a chronic fear of abandonment.

So, on the surface, they might want the promotion or the approval of a new boyfriend, but when they look beneath the surface, they recognize their pain. Even very emotionally healthy teens can experience fears that manifest as superficial desires. They can fear being left out, left behind, or rejected. When they notice these fears, perhaps with your coaching, they can evaluate them. Will a teen really "belong" more anywhere or with anyone because she is holding a phone, or will she feel more isolated and lonely, as do many teens who become dependent on phones to fill the empty spaces in their lives? Will being rich really satisfy my student or offer him security, or will he become anxious about losing what he has? Will others admire him for who he really is or for some false self he portrays to the world?

If our teenagers come to recognize the fears or false assumptions beneath their surface desires, they will become a little more free. They will begin to resist the little lies that make them feel they need to be like everyone else, or that their value depends on the shoes they wear, or how many "likes" they get on their social media posts. They'll begin to resist the urge to follow the crowd mindlessly.

As you invite your teen to search below her surface desires, she might touch on something painful. She may realize she's been avoiding something or playing it safe. Invite her to lean on you; let her look at those fears without your judgment, perhaps without your advice. Give her space to see her deeper desires while she rests in the safety of your love. Point her toward the safety of God's love. As one spiritual director puts it, "God's perfect love casts out fear, leaving us free to desire what is best, not what is expedient or merely safe."[1]

Our deeper longings get to the heart of who we are and what God wants for us. God is not detached from our freedom. When we are in a state of grace, the Holy Spirit moves in us, nudging us toward happiness. Ultimately, all authentic human desires lead to God.[2] We want our desires to be God's desires for us, and we discover his desire for us partly by gradually peeling away the layers of surface, false, or disfigured desires.

Acknowledging Sin

One of our primary duties as parents is to ensure the moral formation of our children. In reality, all humans know right from wrong; the moral law is written into our nature (see CCC 1776). This is called the natural law; these are the things we all know are wrong just because we're human beings. No matter where you grew up or how smart you are, everyone knows certain things are wrong, even if they decide to act against their conscience in these matters.

We don't give our kids their conscience; God gave it to them. Even small children have a natural sense of right and wrong. For example, they know it's wrong to steal or hit (though reminders are always helpful). The *Catechism* calls our conscience our "most secret core" and "sanctuary" (1776). However, because of our fallen human nature and the allure of sin, because we live in a world that has lost its moral compass, our conscience can become obscured. Satan whispers lies in our ear about what is "good"; we can become deaf to our conscience. So, we must guide our children in recognizing, forming, protecting, and respecting their conscience.

Having a well-formed moral conscience prepares our children for later discernment work that requires a humble heart disposed to God's will. Why? Because God would never want them to make a choice that violated what he has already revealed in Scripture or Church Tradition. The Church's moral teaching helps them know which doors are definitely closed to them when making decisions. As part of their moral education, at a minimum, we teach kids the Ten Commandments, the seven deadly sins, and the difference between mortal and venial sins.[3]

Our children will come to understand more clearly why some actions are wrong in particular circumstances as they grow up. In fact, the *Catechism* says our conscience will need educating and forming for our entire lives (see 1784).

Some parents don't like to teach their children about sin; they worry it's too negative and will scar their children with some kind of toxic Catholic guilt. There's a difference between unhealthy guilt — "I'm a bad person" — and healthy guilt — "What I did was wrong." Unhealthy guilt is a feeling that we're bad or damaged even if we've done nothing wrong; we feel guilty for something we didn't do or exaggerate our wrongdoing. Healthy guilt is proportional to the action committed; it serves to move us to make amends and change our behavior. Healthy guilt is a gift, not a mental illness.

I use the virtues every day in my mothering to inspire my children to holy action; I try to help them see the right thing to do, rather than barking "don'ts" at

Freedom to Choose the Good

Your teenager might ask you why she has to follow Church teaching if God created her with the gift of freedom. Shouldn't she be free to choose what is right and wrong for herself? This demonstrates a misunderstanding of the nature of freedom. God gives us the freedom to choose to do what is right or wrong, but we do not have the freedom to define right and wrong. Some things are objectively wrong, and they have been wrong from the beginning of time. God created the world with a particular order, and he created us with a particular end, which is beatitude in heaven. We actually become more free when we follow God's moral law because we move closer to our true end. Nothing creates more chaos in our lives than choosing to defy God's moral law.

them. However, I can't avoid teaching them about the vices (things that are wrong to do). Sin is real. Satan knows it, and he hopes we don't. One of Satan's cunning moves is to lock us into repeating the same sin so that we become enslaved to it. Satan doesn't want us to grow in virtue; he doesn't want us to become skilled in discernment. He wants us to follow our whims and make ourselves into gods. If I teach my kids only about the virtues, they may twist the virtues (like love or kindness) to excuse sinful behavior — "I want to be a loving friend, so I'll support my friend if she wants to sneak out of the house to see her boyfriend." We cannot raise well-formed Christian children without teaching them which choices will cut them off from God and why.

The moral law is not a rigid set of rules meant to ruin our happiness; rather, it frees us so that we can find happiness. "Man is made to live in communion with God in whom he finds happiness: 'When I am completely united to you, there will be no more sorrow or trials; entirely full of you, my life will be complete'" (CCC 45).

On the Stumpers, We Have Mother Church

Even if we have a well-formed conscience, we won't automatically know how to respond to every moral question and dilemma. Our conscience isn't a computer program. Particularly as our children enter the late elementary and teen years, they begin to have more challenging questions about morality. For instance, how do they square our duty to love with the Church's teaching on homosexuality, or the commandment not to kill with our decision to put the family dog down? In these cases, we are called to inform and educate ourselves about the Church's teaching. We are called to discern what is "right and good and discern the will of God expressed in divine law" (CCC 1787).

God has given to the Church the responsibility of *transmitting* his teachings, and we participate in this mission when we evangelize our children. However, parents don't share or participate in the Church's role of *interpreting* revealed truth. The Church's teaching body is called the Magisterium, whose task it is to give "an authentic interpretation of the word of God, whether in its written form [Sacred Scripture] or in the form of Tradition" (CCC 85). The Magisterium has the responsibility of interpreting Scripture, doctrines, and dogmas so that God's people know what is right and wrong. We have an obligation to listen carefully to what the Magisterium says about difficult moral issues. The Church's moral teaching is a light that can guide our children through the wilderness of the modern world, where moral relativism has led to the casual, unquestioning acceptance of grave evils.

As suggested in chapter two, invite your teen to ask her hard questions and arrange those No T.O.T.T. nights. Explore with your teenager what the Church teaches on tough issues that matter to her. Your teen will hear the secular viewpoint on these issues before long, so it's best that she learns from you what the Church really teaches before she encounters a hostile interpretation of the teaching. Teenagers tend to be very idealistic. I do know some teenagers who are fierce apologists for the Faith; they have some introductory training in philosophy and theology. But most teens tend to lack well-developed reasons for what they believe. They believe something because their friends believe it, or a teacher or social media influencer they like said it.

If your teenager expresses an opinion that conflicts with Church teaching, ask her to hold off making up her mind or acting on the opinion until she learns more about the issue from both sides. I would point out the good intention you see in her viewpoint but explain the reasoning behind official Church teaching. So often, our teens' misguided opinions come from a wonderful place of compassion in them, but they lack a nuanced understanding of the issue. For example, if your teenager says she thinks abortion should be legal because a woman might be poor and unable to feed her child, you can recognize your teen's concern for the woman but point out that the ends can't justify the means. Helping a woman is a good goal, but the murder of an innocent child is an evil means to that goal; we have to find a different means to this laudable goal.[4]

M.O.P. Up Sin with Virtue

In *Discipleship Parenting*, I explain how I use virtue training in my mothering. The more our children practice the virtues, the stronger their virtue muscles become, and the easier it becomes to do the virtuous thing. "Striving for virtue transforms not only our children's actions, but also their hearts. They'll not only act nobly, but they'll become truly, deeply noble. The great spiritual masters tell us that the more virtuous a person is, the more liberated and authentically beautiful he is."[5] So we don't want our teenagers to know only the Ten Commandments and the seven deadly sins, as important as they are! We want them to know the countering virtues for these sins. Bishop Robert Barron has a great program called *Seven Deadly Sins, Seven Lively Virtues*, in which he shows the virtues that correct each of the seven deadly sins. For example, the virtue of humility is a correction to pride, and the virtue of forgiveness is a correction to anger. The virtues inspire our teens to reach for personal greatness. Think of the four cardinal virtues — prudence, justice, fortitude, and temperance — and the many human virtues that group around these four, like self-discipline, courage, caring, patience, and responsibility. By practicing the virtues, our teens replace bad habits with good habits.

Because they're still growing up, we remind our teens what these virtues mean, and we take responsibility for helping them practice these virtues. One way to mentor teens in virtue is through what I'll call **M.O.P.** (motivation, obstacles, practice).[6]

When you notice your teen has developed a bad habit, identify the virtue that will correct the habit. Help your teen recognize the **motivations** (the positive reasons) for acquiring the virtue, the **obstacles** preventing him from acquiring the virtue, and how to **practice** the virtue in a particular circumstance.

Let's say your teenager has a bad habit of turning his math homework in late. So, you decide your teen needs to practice the virtue of self-discipline. This is a good example because self-discipline is one of the most important virtues for teenagers to practice as they make the transition from childhood to adulthood. Teenagers have an increasing ability to understand the future benefits of choices they make today, so you can **motivate** your math student by pointing out the benefits of being more self-disciplined about his math homework. He'll be much less stressed, he'll get better grades, and he'll be better prepared for the next level of math. Even more, he'll feel a sense of confidence and pride in his work. Then, help the teen identify the **obstacles** that are keeping him from getting his math homework done. Is his bedroom conducive for study? Does the pinging on his phone distract him? Is his weeknight job getting in the way of studying? Once your teen identifies these obstacles, you can help him come up with solutions to reduce or eliminate them. Finally, help your teen **practice** self-discipline by taking concrete steps to eliminate the obstacles and set goals for when he'll study. Maybe he needs to leave his phone in the kitchen while he studies, and maybe he needs a schedule posted above his study area to remind him about his math study commitment.

When our kids are little, we set goals for them, and we tell them, step-by-step, how to work toward these goals. Teenagers should begin taking ownership of their schedules and responsibilities, but sometimes they need reminders. So, we can give them those reminders, and we can require them to attend to their schedules and goals. We must practice virtue ourselves as we guide our teens in practicing the virtues.

Using Stories to Teach Virtues

Teaching the virtues with an academic approach isn't always fruitful with teenagers, especially if we're too pushy and preachy. Reading fiction aloud to your teens is a great way to teach virtue in a non-threatening or tedious way because you're focusing on the characters in the story rather than the teen. Use stories to present an appealing vision of virtue: Which virtues can we see in a character? What makes the character's actions admirable? At what point in the story does the character face a difficult choice? How does the character make the virtuous choice? We can also use stories to present the unappealing vision of vice in a character who causes destruction to himself and others. Does this character make a choice from which he couldn't recover later? What false assumptions did the character make about this choice? Did the character believe a lie about himself, others, or the world? Did the character present a false front to other characters? What impact did the choice have on other characters? This approach uses the imagination and the emotions to teach valuable lessons about the consequences of our choices and how virtuous habits make it easier to do the right thing in difficult circumstances.

Stories always involve some kind of conflict or struggle, often revealing a limitation in the characters, even virtuous characters. Stories help us to think and talk about the nature of friendship, courage, love, and perseverance. When the characters make poor choices, do they make it right, or do they try to cover up their mistakes? What qualities in the characters does your teen admire or dislike?

You can ask your teen questions about books she's reading on her own or give her a suggested reading list, but it's more fruitful to read the books with her so you have a better sense of what's going on. It's not weird to read aloud to teenagers. Families used to read aloud together in their living rooms every night after dinner. Everyone listened, including the adults. So, connect with your teen by reading aloud to her. Even if she resists initially, just do it. In years to come, she'll remember these moments fondly. I required my teenage daughter to sit with my younger children while I read aloud *Alice in Wonderland* a few years ago. I conceded that she was a bit old for the story, but she was willing to listen. She ended up loving the story so much that she watched the movie version. Of course, you can listen to books on audio together, too, if you prefer.

A few[7] good titles that spark great conversations:

- *Where the Red Fern Grows* by Wilson Rawls teaches the virtues of perseverance and responsibility as the protagonist (Billy) works for two years to save money to buy a pair of hunting dogs. Notice the antagonists, Ruben and Rainie Pritchard, who are nothing but mean, nasty, and vindictive. Ask your teen how these boys might have come to have such hard hearts.
- *To Kill a Mockingbird* by Harper Lee sparks conversation about the virtues of good counsel, loyalty, love, and justice. The book is a coming-of-age story about a little girl, Scout, and her brother, Jem, confronting the ugliness of racism in their small town. Scout's father, Atticus Finch, suffers for his decision to defend a black man who is unjustly accused of a crime. Talk to your teen about situations you've faced when doing the right thing cost you something. Doing the right thing doesn't necessarily make our lives easier, but it makes us more alive and more human.

- *The Hiding Place* by Corrie ten Boom, based on a true story, depicts the horrors of life in a Nazi prison camp. The protagonist and her family hide Jewish people in their home. Eventually, they are caught and imprisoned. This book will spark conversations about the virtues of faith, hope, and forgiveness. If your teen enjoys this book, you might also read aloud *One Day in the Life of Ivan Denisovich* by Aleksandr Solzhenitsyn.
- *The Coral Island* by R.M. Ballantyne teaches the virtues of perseverance and courage. Three teenagers survive a shipwreck and must work together to find food and shelter. Eventually, they must fend off cannibals and pirates! This book inspired *The Lord of the Flies* by William Golding, which most of us read in high school. While Ballantyne's boys must deal with evil characters intruding on their idyllic island, in Golding's version, the evil emerges from within the boys.

The same advice holds true for stories in movies. Every movie has a conflict with different characters responding to the conflict. After you watch a movie as a family, invite reflection and questions. What virtues are demonstrated or missing in the characters' choices? Could your teen identify with any characters? What would your teen do if faced with the same conflict?

Seeking God's Will

I share with my teens a lesson I had to learn the hard way: Seeking and doing God's will leads to increased self-understanding and fulfillment, and avoiding his will sends you in circles and down rabbit holes. Hopefully, they will learn the lesson more quickly than I did. I spent many years chasing what I wanted to do because I simply didn't trust anybody to lead me or protect me. When I finally arrived at a place in my life where I wanted to give up controlling everything, when I wanted to surrender to God's plan for me, it was difficult for me to discern what God really wanted. I wondered, where should I look for God's will? Should I just flip a coin or open my Bible and poke my finger at a verse? What should I do if I can't hear God's voice telling me to do one thing or another? I found Christian discernment principles invaluable in helping me make important decisions or handling difficult situations.

I've discovered that when we follow God's plan for us, we find greater peace and purpose, no matter what life throws our way. This is important for our teens to learn as they approach important forks in the road in the years to come. We want our teens to know that God doesn't leave them alone to navigate life's many choices. Like any loving father, he wants to chat with them and give them advice. God communicates with them in many ways — through his creation, through Scripture, through Church Tradition and teaching, and sometimes through the words of trusted guides. He also communicates with them directly and personally, particularly during prayer and meditation.[8] God helps us reach our supernatural end by guiding us and suggesting the direction we should take in life. He reveals the destination, and he gives us the means to reach it.

You can teach your teen some of these discernment principles. When my older daughter was discerning where to go to college, I watched several of Father Mike Schmitz's videos on discernment, took notes, and made handouts with discussion questions and prayers. My kids found the videos very digestible and helpful. I created mini-retreats and lessons on discernment for them. The principles I'm sharing with you are drawn mostly from these resources.[9]

*God always wills for them to choose
the good, even when it's hard.*

We need to discern God's will when we are choosing between two good and worthy choices, and never between doing the wrong thing and the right thing. For example, we discern whether to become a wife or a religious sister, or whether to spend our weekend with Grandma or our youth group. We don't need to discern whether we should gossip about a friend or steal a parent's credit card! So, this is the foundational rule for teen discernment: It is never God's will for them to sin, no matter how they feel. No matter how much they desire something, no matter what their friends say, no matter how unpopular they will feel if they do or don't do something, God wants them to choose virtue every time.

The first step in spiritual growth is letting go of habitual sin. If our teen smokes pot, sleeps with his girlfriend, abuses his siblings, defies his parents, and refuses to repent of these habits, he will be stuck spiritually. He'll have two warring voices in his life: God will prick his conscience, trying to draw him back home; Satan will try to make him feel very comfortable in his sinful life, planting doubts in his head about what you've taught him about right and wrong.

Growth in discernment always begins here. This is true for every Christian. When we gradually let go of sinful habits, we begin to have the right disposition to hear God's voice guiding us where we need to go. We become increasingly open to whatever God wills; we slowly let go of insisting on our own way; then, we become freer to discern.[10]

They should keep their spiritual ears fine-tuned.

We'll never know God's opinion about an important decision if we never ask him! Many spiritual masters suggest we pray in the following ways when we have an important decision to make.

The Eucharist. One of the graces of the Eucharist is that it awakens in us a desire to respond to God's love for us. Indeed, the Eucharist shapes our desires and longings and increases our self-understanding so that we are better prepared for discernment. It helps us to want only what God wants. For me, the Eucharist opened the door to my reversion to the Church, softening my resistance and stubbornness. Invite your teen to attend Mass and adoration with you, especially when she has an important decision to make.

Sacred Scripture. Praying with Scripture is a time-honored spiritual practice, and it's a very fruitful form of prayer when we're facing important decisions. Pope Leo XIII said, "In the sacred books, the Father who is in heaven comes lovingly to meet His children and talks with them."[11] *God's word is full of great advice!* Your teen might pray the psalms or meditate on the Gospel readings from daily Mass. What is God saying to her through his word; which words or scenes catch her attention or clarify something about her situation? When I first introduce the concept of praying with Scripture to my catechism students, I start with the Gospel of Luke because it deals with themes that seem to resonate with them — the insider v. the outsider, important people v. invisible people. Your teen might read a chapter a day, pausing at passages that strike her in some way.

At least once a year, I lead my children in *lectio divina* ("sacred reading") for several weeks. *Lectio divina* is an ancient form of praying with Scripture through specific stages that draw us deeper into a Scripture passage and invite us to connect personally with the people and events in it. I like to suggest that my kids listen for one word or phrase in the reading that catches their attention; I ask them to meditate on that word or phrase. Sometimes they don't notice anything, and that's okay. Your teen can use the free apps at Sacred Space (sacredspace.ie) or Pray as You Go (pray-as-you-go.org), which will guide him step-by-step through *lectio*, using a Scripture passage from the daily Mass readings. If you want to lead your teen in *lectio*, I've written some free guides for parents to use with their children; the guides work well with children ages five and up.[12]

Daily Examen. The examen is a prayer of reflection on the events of our day, so we can see how God is working in our lives and where he might be leading us. We prayerfully review the day, playing back the events like a movie in our minds. When we notice small gifts and graces that came our way, we recognize them as signs of God's love, and we offer thanks; when we notice we didn't handle a situation in a godly manner, we ask for forgiveness. If your teenager isn't familiar with the examen, Hallow has a good app; God in All Things (godinallthings.com) has morning and evening examens in their audio meditations archive. The examen is a great practice not only when we're discerning a decision but also for growing in our awareness of God's presence in every aspect of our lives.

Silence. In my discussion of emergence in a previous chapter, I explained the importance of solitude for our teens' healthy development. Now I'll make a pitch for silence! Our teenagers are assaulted at all hours by noise. Cars honking, phones dinging, machines grinding, microwaves beeping. And they usually choose the noise over silence. Our teens need more silence for their sanity, let alone their quality discernment.[13] Our teens can't hear God's voice or recognize the stirrings of their own hearts if they don't stop and listen once in a while. If your teen doesn't have enough silence, lead him into it. Announce to your children that you are instituting a noise cleanse. Set aside time each day or week when your home is free of sound pollution — no phones, televisions, computers, microwave ovens, stand mixers.

These practices can form part of a rule of life for your teen's growing faith. As your teen's prayer life grows, his spiritual ears will become increasingly sensitive to God's voice. We have to set aside time on our calendar for God, or we will tend to let it slip. To begin this journey, your teen might spend ten minutes in prayer each day and attend adoration at your parish once a week. His silent prayer will be beautiful and fruitful during adoration. If you don't think your teen is ready to take the initiative in incorporating some of these practices in his week, lead the way by including them in a family rule of life. Use your family rule as a way to guide your older kids and teens in developing their own prayer habits. Teens can seem resistant in the beginning, but something will "go in."

My son Aidan tells me that sometimes one prayer method helps him more than others; he uses what is most "life-giving" for the situation.[14] He may be drawn to the Rosary in one situation or to Eucharistic adoration in another. He says he goes where he is led. He also recommends frequent confession when you are facing a difficult decision, because you not only receive the grace to discern the decision, but "you receive the graces to resist temptation, and you receive strength in the fight against evil."

I should mention that spiritual directors caution us about the limited fruitfulness in spiritual discernment work when the directee is emotionally or psychologically immature. All teens fit this category to some extent, but the most problematic issues occur when the directee has serious emotional problems. When a person has deep emotional wounds or psychological defenses, he may be convinced that he needs to do something or avoid something — some work, person, or experience.[15] For example, if a person struggles with insecure attachment, he may feel drawn to help the poor not because he is called, but because he needs to feel important. Or he may avoid marriage not because he feels called to surrender all for love of God, but because he doesn't want to commit himself to anybody.

Provided our teen is emotionally healthy with a secure attachment status, some spiritual discernment training will be very fruitful. Even if your teen doesn't begin to use the tools of discernment right away, he will have the tools to draw upon when he's ready or willing to use them. With a little understanding of Christian discernment, our teens can begin to notice whether a choice will lead them closer to or further away from God.

Discernment requires movement, but it can be a small movement.

When we have a decision to make, we should begin by gathering information, assessing risks, and weighing advantages and disadvantages. Then we should seek wise counsel from somebody whose advice is valuable in the situation. Our advisors can't make the decision for us, but their insights can help us discern. At some point, we have to make a decision. Sometimes this decision can be a preliminary step in the discernment process; it doesn't have to be an "all-in" kind of decision.

For example, when Aidan was discerning whether or not to apply to seminary, he gathered information on whether it was even possible for a college-level man to enter seminary in our diocese. If the answer was no, then that would have ended the discernment process for a while. But it was possible, so he weighed the advantages and disadvantages of going to seminary directly out of high school or after college. He sought advice from my husband and me, his youth leader at our parish, and our parish priest. He began seeing a spiritual director. He took a big step by applying to both a regular college and to seminary. Our bishop accepted him into the priestly discernment program for our diocese, but he declined to send him to seminary initially. He wanted Aidan to go to college for a year or two to continue his discernment process there. This was more clarity for Aidan on what he should do! You see, sometimes we take a step forward, and God directs us down a particular path on our way to our ultimate destination. After a year, the bishop decided Aidan was ready to enter seminary, and he continues this discernment to this day. He is now a major seminarian (graduate school level), and he will continue to discern, one day at a time, whether or not he is called to the priesthood.

For your teenager, the small step might be to check on audition dates for a play, even if she's not sure she's ready to do it, or she might see how much it would cost to buy a car if she is trying to discern whether to get one. Taking a small step can narrow or clarify our options, and this is part of the discernment process.

Sometimes when we ask, "God, what do you want?" God answers, "Well, what do *you* want?"

When we're trying to make a decision, we can become stuck because we're waiting for a perfectly clear answer, like a bolt of lightning in the sky. Sometimes God wants us to take a small step, as mentioned in the previous principle. At other times, God isn't saying anything because his answer is, "Well what do *you* want to do?" Sometimes the two options are both fantastic, with different benefits and challenges. So God allows us to use our gifts of intellect and will to decide.

If your teen has two great choices, and God is letting her decide, she'll grow spiritually regardless of the choice she makes. Of course, the choices will certainly lead her in different directions, and this is why she should decide wisely. She can take a step toward one of the options. If she discovers she made a mistake, and that this was not the right option for her, it's okay. It's never the end of the world or the end of the road when you are a child of God. Your teen will gain clarity and self-understanding, and she can move in a different direction.

Following God's will does not mean you will avoid discomfort or suffering.

Because our teens are still immature, they may assume that if they are uncomfortable, they must be "off track" and failing to follow God's will completely. They assume the Christian life equals the comfy life, devoid of pain or suffering; we follow the Christian path to optimize our comfort. So, if our teen is anxious about studying for a test, she may assume it's God's will for her to take an easier academic track in high school. After all, would a loving God really want her to be anxious? If our teen's best friend disapproves of her decision not to attend a co-ed sleepover (which is a "thing" in some schools), she may jump to the conclusion that God wants her to attend the sleepover to love and support her friend. She assumes "loving her neighbor" is the same as making her neighbor comfortable. I remember having thought processes like these when I was a teen and young adult. It's faulty thinking.

Doing the right thing and following God's will is not a ticket to a cloud of ease. In fact, it often brings with it conflict, discomfort, and loss. We want our teens to know that they can't avoid suffering, but they grow in virtue and holiness through these trials. Doing evil also brings suffering; we fall deeper into chaos, cutting ourselves off from God. As the Apostle Peter tells us, it is better to suffer for doing good than to suffer for doing evil — because indeed we will suffer if we make the wrong choice, acting against the divine law:

> But even if you do suffer for righteousness' sake, you will be blessed. Have no fear of them, nor be troubled, but in your hearts reverence Christ as Lord. Always be prepared to make a defence to anyone who calls you to account for the hope that is in you, yet do it with gentleness and reverence; and keep your conscience clear, so that, when you are abused, those who revile your good behavior in Christ may be put to shame. For it is better to suffer for doing right, if that should be God's will, than for doing wrong. (1 Peter 3:14–17)

Being a follower of Christ isn't about "being nice." Yes, Christ calls us to love, but love is working for the good of the person, not telling them what they want to hear or making them comfortable. It's hard to go against the crowd. Doing the right thing or refusing to participate in evil makes you unpopular in some crowds. It's especially hard for teenagers who have a wobbly sense of self. As I've said before, if our teens are too immature to handle the temptations or conflict in particular situations, we have to take responsibility and protect them from those situations.

Your teen may be more or less interested in these principles from one day to the next. You can introduce the principles, offer reminders on occasion in particular circumstances, and try the principles yourself, modeling discernment for your teen. Teenagers pay attention to our example.

Discerning True Friendship

We know from our own experience that we tend to become like the people we spend the most time with, and research bears this out.[16] Our closest friends influence our perceptions of the world, what we consider valuable, and even how we feel about particular people and events. It matters who our friends are, and it certainly matters who our *teens'* friends are. When our kids are little, we tend to choose their friends for them, and unless they are peer-oriented, their friends tend to have minimal impact on their viewpoints or choices. Something shifts in the teen years, though. Even if we have a close, warm relationship with our teens, we should be mindful of who their friends are. We simply can't underestimate the power of peer pressure to shape our teens' hearts and lives.

A recent Virginia Tech study looked at whether teenagers are influenced by *positive* peer pressure as strongly as negative peer pressure. [17] We already knew from copious research that

teenagers are more likely to use drugs and engage in dangerous behavior when they are with friends who are doing these
things. Even perfectly sensible teenagers sometimes make terrible choices that we could never imagine them making when
apart from their peers. The Virginia Tech team wondered whether teens could be influenced as much by risk-averse friends. In
other words, would kids make good choices when peers around
them make good choices? They discovered that teens who tend
to care about their peers' opinions of them are more likely to
follow their peers' choices, whether these choices are positive or
negative, safe or dangerous. If you know your teen tends to care
too much about what her friends think of her, you have to provide opportunities for her to meet kids with good values, and
you have to step in and redirect friendships that are damaging.

The study also found that teens in the "good kid" crowd were
more likely to follow a peer making safe choices. This should
give you comfort if you have raised your children with boundaries around behavior and lessons in virtue. Your kids are more
likely to flock together with other kids making good choices.
Let's encourage them to stick together!

We are responsible for our teenagers until they are mature
enough to take responsibility for themselves. We must take the
lead in ensuring we know who our teens' friends are. Think about
your teen's circle of friends. I mean, really, *who are they*? What are
their interests? What are their favorite foods? What sort of traditions do they enjoy at home? While you don't need to give them
the third degree, express genuine curiosity about them. Invite
them to join your family for game night or Friday night pizza.
Not only is this just a smart thing to do to remain engaged in
your teen's life, but you will be opening your heart to another
child. Maybe yours is the only Christian family this child knows.

You may discover some things about your teen's friends that
are less than ideal, but unless the friend is leading your teen into

a life of sin or unwilling to respect your family's values, I would give the friend a chance. If the friend is encouraging damaging ideas and behavior, you will have to limit your teen's time with this friend. While we don't want to reject a young person in our community who is in trouble, we can certainly set and enforce boundaries around how our kids spend time with these youth, particularly when we know they may encourage our kids to make bad choices. We also have to be honest with ourselves about our teen's temperament and maturity. Is he confident in peer groups? Can he speak his mind? Does he have a strong sense of self so that he is less likely to mirror his peers' choices just to fit in?

Three Types of Friendships

As our teens mature, we can guide them in recognizing the qualities of a good friend. We all tend to have three types of friendships: friendships of utility, friendships of pleasure, and friendships of virtue. These three categories were first explored in ancient philosophy and taken up later by many Catholic theologians, including Thomas Aquinas.

Friendships of utility are the most superficial type of friendship. They're hardly friendships at all, really. These relationships rely on how useful or beneficial the friends are to each other. These are shallow friendships that tend to end when our circumstances or needs change. Are friendships of utility wrong? Well, it depends. In adulthood, some friendships of utility are inevitable. Some professions require networking for success; you cultivate some friendships strictly for business purposes. You don't know these people well, and frankly, you aren't inclined to know them any more than you already do.

Our teenagers might have friends like this on sports teams or school projects. They're happy to see these friends during practice or school, but they quickly forget about them when the season or the project ends. I think social media "friendships" with people we have never met also tend to be like this. As long as we are not exploiting the other person or diminishing the person's dignity in any way, friendships of utility are just a part of life. But we want our kids to know that friendships of utility can never meet their deep need for connection and intimacy.

Friendships of utility become immoral when the friends treat one another as objects or one friend somehow exploits the other. The hook-up culture prevalent in youth and young adult circles is degrading — these young people use each other like they would a chair. They are quite frank that their sexual partners don't mean anything to them. So the other person is just a body to use for satisfying their own urges. This is wrong. We want our kids to know that they shouldn't allow themselves to be treated this way, and they should never treat others this way, even if it's accepted in their schools and peer circles.

Most of our teens' friendships fall into the second category: **friendships of pleasure**. This is a more admirable type of friendship than friendships of utility because our teen genuinely enjoys the other person's company. The whole purpose of the friendship is to have fun together, and the friendship lasts so long as the fun lasts. Depending on how teens spend time with these friends, they are of more or less concern to parents. Maybe they play video games every weekend, go fishing in the neighborhood lake, or explore fashion and makeup tips. This isn't a problem as long as you're okay with these activities. Of course, if our teens are doing immoral or self-destructive things with these friends, we have to be the adult and lead our teens out of the behavior. And if the friend is hostile to our family's faith or exhibits any bullying-type behavior, we have to step in.

These pleasure-type friendships rarely have depth. Healthy teenagers are capable of attaching at all six levels of attachment; they yearn to be vulnerable with somebody, but this isn't safe with most peers. Our teens discover before long that they need to be prudent about what they share with such friends because the friends may use the information against them or withdraw from the friendship when our teens express emotional vulnerability. Many of our teens are heartbroken when friends begin distancing themselves after they face a personal crisis and need support. But these friendships of pleasure are short-lived for this very reason.

The most genuine type of friendship is the **friendship of virtue**. We want our teenagers to understand this type of friendship and recognize its rarity, even among adults. In this friendship, we value the friend not because we can get something from him, but because we admire his character; we have some shared ideal that we explore or work toward together. In fact, we are more likely to realize the ideal because we have this friend in our lives. As St. Maximilian Kolbe put it, "God sends us friends to be our firm support in the whirlpool of struggle. In the company of friends, we will find strength to attain our sublime ideal." These people help us see what matters most in life; our lives seem more beautiful and meaningful because of them. In the first two types of friendships, we tend to focus on what we can get out of the friendship, but in a friendship of virtue, we seek the best for our friend even if it's inconvenient or hurts us in some way. For example, we support our friend in pursuing an opportunity even if it means we won't see them as much anymore. Virtuous friends sacrifice for the good of the other friend.

If you want to provide examples for your teen of great friendships of virtue, we have many stories in Sacred Scripture and saints' lives. Think of Ruth and Naomi in the Book of Ruth. Ruth was married to Naomi's son. After the son dies, Naomi, a widow, tells Ruth to go home to her own people and remarry. Ruth refuses to leave Naomi's side. She journeys back to Bethlehem with Naomi, a land where she is a stranger. She loves Naomi so much that she works day and night to provide for Naomi, and Naomi loves and guides Ruth in return. The friendship between St. Basil the Great and St. Gregory Nazianzen is equally remarkable for their loyalty to one another and their mutual pursuit of sanctity. In a sermon, Gregory said of his friendship with Basil:

> Our single object and ambition was virtue, and a life of hope in the blessings that are to come; we wanted to withdraw from this world before we departed from it. With this end in view we ordered our lives and all our actions. We followed the guidance of God's law and spurred each other on to virtue. If it is not too boastful to say, we found in each other a standard and rule for discerning right from wrong.[18]

As these great friendships reveal, when we have a virtuous friend, we can journey toward a transcendent destination; we strive together and encourage one another to grow in holiness. We are willing to suffer in helping one another reach this destination. We will meet few people in our lifetimes with whom we have this kind of rapport and trust. We can conclude that for somebody to be such a worthy friend, they must possess virtue and enough maturity to prioritize others' needs over their own. We have to be able to trust them with our hearts.

We also want our teenagers to know that some friendships in their lives will begin as friendships of utility or pleasure, but they will deepen over time and become friendships of virtue. You don't know when you meet somebody that this will happen; you can't force it. And friendships of virtue always include some aspects of utility and pleasure. Virtuous friends rely on each other for practical things, and they should have shared interests that make life more enjoyable.

I think it's quite rare for teenagers to possess the maturity necessary to attain much more than a neophyte-level friendship of virtue. But when two teenagers want to grow in faith, when they have a sense of shared mission, it's certainly possible, especially in the late teen years. I believe my son Aidan had such a friendship when he was in high school. Aidan had many good friends when he was younger, but they were definitely friendships of pleasure. After all, they were kids. They built Lego together and hit each other with lightsabers! But when he was about seventeen, Aidan met two Catholic teens, Joey and Gabe, who were a year or two older than he was. Aidan, Joey, and Gabe prayed together, attended adoration, and explored their faith. They challenged one another and held one another accountable, morally and spiritually. They were iron sharpening iron (see Prv 27:17). Together they were stronger in their faith than they would have been apart. This was a great friendship. I am confident that their friendship changed all of them for the better. Of course, they were relatively young. When any of them got into a jam, they turned to their parents for help. But I think those three young men experienced what it's like to stand together with worthy companions, all donned in the armor of Christ.

Our teens will likely have some friends of pleasure who are good-hearted and caring, and our teen and the friend will lean on one another on occasion, but they probably lack the maturity necessary to take real risks in the friendship. So, they will have some friendships that have qualities of virtue but remain mostly undeveloped. These experiences are still valuable for our kids, and these are good friends. Our teens may also have some friends from their earlier childhood who begin making bad choices in the teen years, or our teen and the friend begin to drift apart because their interests change. It's painful for our teenagers to face the reality that they have outgrown a friendship and need to move on. We can encourage them to continue praying for their friend and checking on their well-being occasionally.

Maybe this is all too philosophical for the average teen's interest, but it's still helpful for parents to understand. The bottom-line message for our teens: There are bad friends, acceptable friends, and great friends. At a minimum, our teens should understand that no real friend would ask them to compromise their values or beliefs. No real friend would pressure them to do something they regret later. We want our teenagers to know that the greatest friends they'll ever have in life will have a strong sense of purpose, a growing faith life, and an empathic heart. They won't have many friends like this. Most of their friends will just want to hang out and have fun. These friends will tend to come and go with the seasons, and this is okay.

FRIENDSHIP QUALITIES		
Bad Friends	**Acceptable Friends**	**Great Friends**
spend time together doing sinful and harmful things	spend time together enjoying a mutual interest	spend time together having fun but also pursuing virtue
hostile to your faith	supportive of your faith even if they aren't interested in it	share your passion for your faith and want to explore it with you
disrespectful to their parents; encourage you to lie to your parents	respectful to their parents; assume you will follow your parents' rules	respectful to parents; understand obedience as a virtue
hurt you emotionally; bully you and call it "teasing"; belittle your beliefs or family	don't nourish you emotionally but don't hurt you; respect your boundaries	caring; willing to sacrifice for others; emotionally safe
won't allow you to have other friends; jealousy	comfortable with you having other friends, but wouldn't speak up if a friendship was harmful to you	encourage you to have other friends; speak up if a friendship seems damaging

Teenagers receive training in driving cars and studying for standardized tests, but they are rarely exposed to topics like these that help them understand the nature of wisdom. These discernment tools sink in deeper as our teens mature, and indeed these tools foster maturity. Initially, our kids will probably barely get some of these lessons and messages, but with patience, modeling, and reminders, they will come to see how their choices each day shape their characters and their lives.

Reflection and Direction

- Have a family meeting and chat about the importance of occasional silence in human well-being. Ask your kids how often they sit in complete silence without any devices or other technology. Share your own experience and perhaps your discomfort with silence. Brainstorm ways your family can have mini silent retreats — periods of time in your week or areas of your home where you observe silence. Have follow-up meetings to see how it went for everyone. Be creative! Maybe you can incorporate silent games and quiet crafts during your silent retreats.
- Reflect on your own friendships past and present. Can you identify one or two people in each friendship category: friends of utility, pleasure, and virtue? Did you ever have friends who hurt you or encouraged you to do things you knew were wrong? Talk to your teen about these friends as a way to open up a conversation about the importance of wholesome friendships.

6
Managing Challenges While Protecting Your Relationship

O, Divine Master, grant that I may not so much
seek to be consoled as to console, to be understood
as to understand, to be loved as to love.
— from the Prayer of St. Francis of Assisi

The Big Picture

- Handling your teen's emotional flooding without drowning
- Talking to your teen so she hears what you say
- Navigating conflict with your teen without losing her heart

In Minnesota, where I was born and where most of my extended family still lives, there is a fast-moving type of summer storm called a derecho. While rare, derechos can come out of nowhere when the air is hot, ripping through unsuspecting towns with ferocity. You know where I'm going with this! Just about every parent of an adolescent has occasional "derecho days" with their teen. We can be caught off guard by our teen's sudden volatility, sarcasm, or nastiness, even when we enjoyed a close, warm relationship previously — maybe an hour before! Because these teen storms may come with a lot of attacking energy, they may touch our own wounds and weaknesses, causing us to react impulsively rather than respond productively.

In this book, we're thinking about how we transmit faith to teenagers. Inter-relational conflict is relevant because it can drive teens away from their faith mentors or foster a resentment that stifles spiritual growth. In this chapter, I want to share a few insights that I've gleaned over the years about managing conflict with my teenagers. Frequently, the tension has been unavoidable, and my job has been to hold the relationship steady through the storm. Some days I feel like I'm barely controlling the rudder. Other days I blow it. I have often exacerbated tensions with my teenagers because of my own anxieties and assumptions. So, I am not writing from the perspective of a mother who has it all together every day. But I do think I see better than I once did the nature and source of parent-teen conflict, and I've discovered a few ways to navigate through it without doing too much damage to my relationship with my teens.

Making Room for Emotions

As I noted in an earlier chapter, while it can be challenging (really, *really* challenging), it's important for our teens' development that we make room for all their emotions, not just the ones we like to see. If we aren't comfortable with all their emotions, our teens won't be either. They may reject these emotions in themselves and others, which will hinder the unfolding of their attachment potential. If God gave us emotions, they must have some purpose in human flourishing. I talk about this purpose at length in my first book, *Discipleship Parenting*.[1] Briefly, without the discipline of the rational mind, our emotions can lead us astray; feelings do not always reveal reality. On the other hand, without the energy of our emotions, our wills can become rather wooden: We may do the right thing by formula rather than from the heart. Ideally, our emotions and our rational minds work together to move us toward greater virtue and perfection.

If you remember anything from this chapter, I want you to remember this: Conflict with your teen is not necessarily a sign that you have done something wrong or need to fix something. Yes, sometimes parents need to take action or solve a problem. Still, it's possible what you're looking at in your teen is the inevitable emotional intensity of adolescent development. In these situations, our only job is to maintain the relational invitation to our teen while they figure things out or calm down. Because teenagers are usually the same size as adults, we might assume teenagers should behave like adults. However, there is at least one significant difference between an adult and a teenager: the brain.

The teen brain has a hyperactive amygdala (the emotional center of the brain), so they frequently experience emotional flooding. Your teen can understand abstract concepts and make logical connections in his schoolwork because his prefrontal cortex is maturing. However, the prefrontal cortex is not well-connected to the amygdala in the teen brain. As a result, sometimes teens feel out of control emotionally because the prefrontal cortex doesn't "talk back" to the amygdala. Most of us adults can talk ourselves down when we experience emotional flooding, but teens often feel trapped in their emotions; they believe their emotions represent reality. So, your teen can solve your Sudoku puzzle, but he might throw the pencil across the room if he makes a mistake. Fortunately, emotional flooding usually improves dramatically by the early twenties. I am not making excuses for bad behavior. Teens who experience emotional flooding deserve our understanding when they're legitimately overwhelmed because they may have no control over the flooding. Sometimes they need us to hold steady while they hold on to us for balance. But, like all of us, teens can be rude and disrespectful even when they are fully capable of making better choices. Teens may require reminders about the virtues of patience and respect.

Don't assume that the way your teen handles crises or conflict today will be the way he handles it in the future. The feeling brain and the rational brain should eventually work together to temper our teen's will so that he's capable of doing the right thing for the right reasons at the right time. But during adolescence, this internal machinery is not linked up very well. The temptation is to lash out at or punish our teenagers, but the best way to handle this problem is to draw the teen in closely with your shepherd's crook. We must hold them closer instead of pushing them away and intentionally guide them instead of giving up on them.

We can mentor our teens in expressing their emotions respectfully, but we should never shame them for having emotions. We can prohibit behavior (*you can't hit*) but never feelings (*you can't feel angry*). In particular, we can guard against canceling their angry, disappointed, or sad feelings. These are the three emotions that tend to put parents off, mainly because our teens frequently lack balance and perspective when expressing them. Is it okay for our teenagers to scream and slam doors when they're angry? No, it's not okay. But it *is* okay for them to feel angry. (Unless it's simmering resentment or rage, which can be sinful.)

A few gentle reminders go a long way. "It's okay to be angry, but I can't permit you to call me names. It's not good for you or me." You can also ask your teen to revise his rude or demanding statements: "It's hard for me to hear you when you use that tone. Please ask me again later when you're ready to ask more politely." When I have to redirect like this, I try to follow up almost immediately with an invitation or reminder that the relationship is okay: "I was about to have a bowl of ice cream. Want to join me?" Recall the M.O.P. of virtue training: What will **motivate** your teen to acquire the virtue that will counter an inappropriate emotional expression, what **obstacles** prevent him from acquiring that virtue, and how can he **practice** the virtue in specific circumstances? If your teen recognizes that slamming doors will not work in his long-term friendships, he will be motivated to work on self-control to counter that habit.

Again, no matter the root cause of the emotional turmoil, our job is to maintain our invitation to our teen while he moves through it. In truth, we don't always like being around our teenagers. In these moments, we trust God to raise us above our own frailty so that we can stay in the lead as we continue inviting and protecting our relationship. This is heroic mothering and fathering.

When Emotions Seem Stuck

Some kids become stuck in their hard emotions — they lose their soft, caring feelings and become mired in bitterness or grief. Sometimes they don't want to face their hurts or losses; maybe the emotions are too raw or overwhelming. Build emotion "decloggers" into your family routine. Praying with the Psalms as a family is one option. The Psalms express just about every human emotion from anguish to jealousy to love to regret. Pray a Psalm, then ask your kids what the Psalm is about. Your kids might want to put the Psalm into their own words, perhaps in a prayer journal. Here are a few themes in the Psalms that might help your teen face her feelings:

- Feeling anxiety or fear: Psalms 69 and 88
- Feeling anger: Psalms 25 and 35
- Feeling betrayed: Psalms 7 and 41

Storytelling is another declogger we should build into our family culture. In the last chapter, I shared how I use stories (in novels and movies) to teach my kids about the virtues. Storytelling also loosens up stuck feelings. The great thing about stories is that they help our children face their fears, sadness, doubts, anger, or failures without these emotions or experiences being "too close." This has been true for all human beings for millennia: We use stories to deal with hard stuff. Because a story is about somebody else, it helps us face our inner conflicts and personal struggles in a non-threatening, manageable way. This is why intuitive cultures allow children to read scary fairy tales, which we often sanitize in the West, where we want to protect our children from anything unsettling. Human beings have always processed hard emotions and difficult experiences through stories.

I recommend reading aloud to your teens. If they're too fidgety to sit and listen, they can work on a quiet activity (knitting, drawing, building models) while you read. Any of the titles mentioned in the last chapter would be great for declogging emotions. A few others: *Homeless Bird* by Gloria Whelan and *The Book Thief* by Markus Zusak (some profanity; also available on film).

Communication Dos and Don'ts

With all the pressures on them from peers and society, our teens need at least one trusted adult they can confide in. We want to make it easy for them to open up to us. Over the years, I've learned some dos and don'ts for making it safe for my teens to talk to me. These are communication basics that apply when you're navigating conflict with anybody. Sometimes I do the don'ts and don't do the dos, but I'm gradually growing because of God's grace and mercy.

Do Let Them Talk

As I admit elsewhere in this book, when I hear my teen say something that concerns me, I tend to take over the conversation. Perhaps I think they're about to make a wrong choice, or they parrot a viewpoint I know they picked up from a questionable source. So, I tend to interrupt them and begin dominating the conversation so I can fix the problem. This urge within me is typically rooted in fear — fear that my teens will be hurt in some way, either by somebody else or by one of their choices. I over-advise and lecture because I'm trying to save them, but I have to step back and instead empower them to build

Rules for Communicating with Teenagers

- Do let them talk.
- Don't take things personally.
- Don't assume the worst.
- Do lighten up.

their own lives. That's my job as their mom. So, I'm getting better about buttoning my lip and paying attention to what my teens say.

If you're like me and feel a strong impulse to share your opinions when your teen is trying to talk, here's a helpful tip I learned in another parenting book: Rephrase and repeat what she says instead of advising.[2] When we give advice or try to direct our teens too soon, we tend to focus on how *we* feel and what *we* think, but in the teen years, we want to help our teen recognize what *she* thinks and feels so she learns how to come up with solutions and handle problems herself. For example, if your teen shares with you that her best friend said something hurtful about her on social media, instead of giving advice or taking over ("She was never a good friend anyway" or "I'm calling her mother"), mirror your teen's emotions or frame her thoughts for her ("Wow, that must have surprised you" or "You must be wondering whether or not you can trust her"). When you take this approach, you help your teen recognize the issue and face her feelings about it. You also keep her talking; she's less likely to shut down than if you start bombarding her with advice. If she wants advice, do give your perspective, but you can still help her identify the problem and come up with solutions, or help her clarify her questions and where to find answers. Similarly, while we don't want to grill our teens, it's okay to ask questions like "What were you thinking when she said that?" or "What do you think you'll do next?" These curiosity-style questions are non-threatening and non-judgmental and tend to move the conversation forward with teens because you're focusing on their reaction instead of your own. Be a partner in the conversation instead of the director.

There will be a point where you can share your perspective and remind your teen about rules and expectations. Often my problem is my timing. Usually, some things need to be said, but I don't need to say them immediately. Sometimes my teen needs a sounding board and breather first.

Don't Take Things Personally

Don't become defensive if the way your teen says something stings a little. Sometimes teenagers aren't very tactful, especially when they're upset. They can express themselves too forcefully, and it hurts. There will be a time to guide the teen in responsible, productive expression of their frustration and anger, but at that moment when the explosive feelings are coming at us, it's better to focus on the issue they're upset about rather than their lousy delivery. We can practice the virtue of mercy by giving them a little wiggle room in the manners department. Sometimes I feel hurt because of my own issues and not because of what my teens say. In such situations, I need to lean on God and ask for mercy for myself. When I notice my mind percolating and resisting my teens' words, I say a quick prayer like, "God, I release this into your care. It's too big for me."

Do resist the urge to bite back in response to your teen's criticisms of you. It's tough to listen to a teenager complaining about your faults, especially when she doesn't say it very diplomatically. But if there is some truth in the complaint, admit that you're not perfect. Ask questions about her points if you're unsure where she's coming from, but try to avoid defensiveness, which tends to ignite a cycle of criticism and defensiveness on both sides.

Don't Assume the Worst

Don't immediately assume the worst about your teen until you gather the facts and hear her side of the story. Not long ago, I received an email informing me that one of my teenagers had missed the first day of one of her online classes. She was still sleeping when this email came through. I could feel myself ruminating about the situation. *Why can't she keep her schedule straight? Here she is still sleeping, and she's supposed to be in class.* My stewing continued, and before long, I was pretty angry, rehearsing what I would say to her when she woke up. Thankfully, I resisted the temptation to blast her when she emerged from her room. Together, we pieced together what had happened. It turned out most of the students were not in class that morning because few of the students received the teacher's announcement that he was moving the class start date a week earlier to accommodate a scheduling conflict he had later in the semester. So, my teen was not the only student who slept in that day! I was grateful that I took the time to hear her explanation before accusing her of being irresponsible.

Of course, sometimes our teens do mess up; sometimes they are irresponsible. In these moments, we want to remember the attachment root of loyalty. Our message should be "I'm on your side," even if our teen made a mistake. Not "I agree with your choice," but "I'm with you." Our tone of voice can communicate that if their behavior is bad enough, the relationship with us will be damaged or even end. "I'm done"; "I can't take it anymore"; "I give up." This is placing responsibility for the relationship in our teen's lap. We need them to know with confidence that there is nothing they can do that will make us stop loving them.

We can be loyal without making excuses for our teen's choices or pretending the mistake didn't happen. How do we do this? By making it crystal clear that even when our teen makes a mistake, she's still our kid, and we'll help her figure out a way through the consequences of these choices. Also, being on our teen's side doesn't mean we take sides. If our teen has hurt somebody, we want her to take responsibility and make it right. If our teen has a conflict with a sibling, we don't have to take sides. In such situations, being on our teen's side means we listen to her perspective and help her come up with a solution for how she'll handle the problem. We don't fix the problem for her. We can also recognize the positive intentions in a teen's poor choices. Sometimes our teens are trying to stretch their wings, trying to be nice, trying to avoid rocking the boat, and they find themselves knee-deep in trouble. Good intentions can never excuse wrong actions, but letting your teen know that you recognize her good intentions will keep her heart soft even as she faces the consequences of her choices.

Do Lighten Up

Finally, have fun! The teen years can be challenging, yes, but teenagers are also funny and intriguing. I came to my mothering vocation with many weaknesses and areas of blindness, but one strength I brought with me into this vocation is a sense of playfulness. I don't take myself too seriously; I laugh easily, even when facing obstacles or tragedy. It's a perhaps odd trait, and I think it annoys some people, but it has served me well in my relationship with my kids, especially my teens. My default tone with them is lightness. We tease each other, have punching matches, play practical jokes, arm wrestle, have water balloon fights, and pass on comical stories from our day. Recently my teen was having a hard day, so I did the 1980s running man dance in front of her door to cheer her up. I can also do a great moon walk as long as I'm wearing the right socks. I am sure my playful nature makes me more approachable to my teens. When tensions do surface with my kids, the fundamental connection is there.

Such shenanigans may not be your cup of tea, but you don't have to do what I do; find a lighthearted tone with your teens that feels natural for you. I would say if our default tone is fault-finding, warning, and bossing, our teens will eventually tune us out and view us as somebody they have to tolerate periodically. Teens sometimes merely manage their parents while they're looking for the nearest exit.

What I'm talking about here is our basic relational tone with our teens — our words, our attitude, and our outlook. Beyond

Key Insight: Our Teens Will Continue Maturing in Adulthood!

Sometimes minor conflicts escalate with my teens because I'm anxious to get them to behave in a more civilized or socially acceptable manner. I imagine them in college leaving their dirty underwear on the bathroom floor. I panic and try to shove the teen a little more quickly through the maturity shoot. I say things like, "You want to be treated like a grown-up, but you leave your clothes on the floor like a toddler. What if you have a roommate someday? You have to be more considerate." My kids just feel judged and hurt. Our teenagers will mature a lot between now and when they are independent adults. Even then, they will be works in progress. They'll make mistakes and have some bad habits to work on, just as we do. Eighteen is the end of childhood, but it's only the beginning of adulthood. Our kids will continue learning and growing for the rest of their lives.

this, we want to make time to hang out with our teens regularly. We build and protect rapport with our teens by having plenty of spontaneous and planned fun times with them. Spending all of our time together as a family working through our to-do list eventually stifles the connection, as it does in all our relationships.

Common Sources of Parent-Teen Conflict

Parents and their teens might butt heads about anything, including the definition of "doing the dishes" (which seems not to include pots and pans in my house) or the best place to store clean laundry (the floor seems unreasonable to me, but a few of my teens disagree). Here I'd like to give you some insights and guidance in navigating some particularly challenging sources of parent-teen conflict.

Failure to Follow Through

When kids are little, they think chores are fun. "Can I load the dishwasher?!" "I wanna vacuum, Mom!" But in the teen years, our kids seem to develop memory loss. They forget to load the dishwasher or vacuum, even when you remind them (ten times). When I had issues with my teens following through on chores, commitments, homework, etc., sometimes it was partly my fault. Here are some of the ways I contributed to the problem:

- I made a chore chart or similar plan, but I didn't enforce it consistently, so my teenagers figured it wasn't important. If I don't follow through, how can I expect my teens to follow through? I love making charts, grids, and schedules, complete with color coding and coordinating office supplies, but I am less successful at keeping track of all my big plans! I need to provide routines and rules, but I also need to have clear expectations about follow-through. This is a recurring issue in my mothering, but I'm working on it. I know my whole family does better when we have a consistent routine, and my teenagers are more likely to complete tasks when my expectations are clear and consistent. Our family habits directly impact our teenagers' habits as they leave the nest. By encouraging family follow-through, our teenagers eventually develop a sense of ownership over their daily routines and responsibilities.

- I nagged my teenagers or harshly commanded them to do something, so they tuned me out. Some teens are naturally good-natured and take our bossiness with a grain of salt; other teens need us to be more diplomatic. Instead of barking, "Take out the garbage NOW!," it's more productive to be firm and politely measured. "Hey, buddy, I noticed the garbage is still here." You're just making an observation and giving the teen a chance to solve the problem. It also helps to offer choices. "I noticed the garbage is still here. Wanna take it out now or after dinner?" Another tip: Our teens are less likely to freeze us out when we "collect" them first before giving a reminder or making a request. We all collect naturally in our relationships: We greet people, engage their eyes, ask them how they're doing, inquire what they're up to, ask if they need anything, and so on. Collecting rituals are part of every civilized culture, but we sometimes forget our manners with our teens. Our kids deserve our manners as much as strangers do! We're more likely to engage cooperation and follow-through in our teens if we make a habit of collecting them regularly. The more prickly the teen, the more important collecting becomes in our parenting toolbox.

- I blabbered on until my teenagers got annoyed. I do this sometimes when I'm nervous, but I'm learning to get to the point a little more quickly. I won't say any more about that!

One important developmental task of the teen years is learning how to set goals and meet them. In guiding our teens in ordering their choices, we can give them a positive standard to aspire toward rather than scaring them with warnings and annoying them with nagging. For example, instead of warning your teen not to be lazy, inspire her with the virtue of responsibility. You can do this with your whole family, so your teen doesn't feel you're picking on her. One summer, my family had "a virtue of the week." I posted a definition for the virtue, and all week we talked about how to practice the virtue and how it benefits our relationships and spiritual lives. You can do something like this with the virtue of responsibility. Explain to your kids that when you have a responsible character, others can trust you to follow through on your commitments, show up on time, and do your part. Responsible people don't make excuses when they make mistakes or blame others when they don't follow through. As a result, they are more successful and have greater peace of mind.

Sometimes our teenagers also need to experience the logical consequences of their choices. If they haven't finished their chores, they aren't free to go out with friends to the movies; if they fail to turn in homework on time, they may need to give up sports practices for a semester. Will this create conflict? Yes. It's okay. Sometimes doing the right thing for our kids provokes some pushback, but if the attachment is strong, they'll continue following you. We can keep walking forward with our shepherd's staff. We're in the lead no matter how cranky the sheep are!

Resistance to Faith

You're reading this book because your faith matters to you. You've found something in the Church worth passing on to your children. So, it can be painful and frustrating when your teenagers push back against your deepest-held beliefs about God or the Church. The good news is your kids absorb your faith, values, and practices more than you might realize, at least if they know these things matter to you. Living your faith vibrantly in front of your children is a strong predictor of their affection for the faith in adulthood; but that may not give you much comfort in the moment when your teen refuses to get up to go to Mass.

Some parents remark that they would never "force" their kids to go to Mass because religion is a personal choice. I talked about this viewpoint in the introduction. There I explained why I give my kids choices in morally neutral matters but not in matters of faith or morals. Another important reminder: Many things that will become a personal choice when my kids are adults are my responsibility when they're kids. When they're adults, they'll have a personal choice about whether they'll go to their grandparents' house for dinner, but while I'm responsible for them, they go to Grandpa and Grandma's no matter their opinions about it. When they're adults, they will choose what they eat, too, but for now, I'm responsible for feeding them. Just as I would never let them eat ice cream for dinner, I wouldn't let them miss out on Mass. Just as some teens lack an appreciation for the nutritional value of broccoli, some teens lack an appreciation for the spiritual value of prayer or the graces of the sacraments. I wouldn't allow my kids to skip Mass, in particular, because there we encounter the Eucharist through which we participate in Christ's Paschal Mystery more intensely than in any other way, except perhaps martyrdom.[3] Our teens are armed for battle through our family faith practices, and they need the protection mightily. So, I require my kids to do many things they'd rather not do because I'm the grown-up, and it's on me to keep them safe, feed them, clothe them, and provide them with a solid moral foundation. It's on me to introduce them to people who will get them where they need to go. This includes God.

With that defense out of the way, I'd like to share some thoughts about how best to respond to resistance to faith in your home, should the issue arise. First, talk with your teen. Ask her why she doesn't want to go to Mass or participate in your family prayers or other devotions. What's on her mind? Giving teens the floor shows them that we respect them and care about their perspectives. They feel heard while we gain valuable insights into the source of the problem. This insight is critical for clarifying whether you're dealing with a faith issue or a relationship issue.

Sometimes what seems like rebellion is a natural part of the faith maturing process. Recall that in late adolescence, teens who have strong religious affections and a sense of belonging in their parishes quite naturally transition into a searching stage of faith where they ask questions and may experience doubts about God and the Church. They need to wrestle with and maybe occasionally critique what they have received from us as they move through this phase of faith development. Without permission to ask the questions, their faith lives will sputter out. Admittedly, some teens are more combative than others when asking their questions, and sometimes it's emotionally and mentally exhausting helping them find answers. But if they'll trust us to get them through it, their faith will grow. There may be some bumps in the road that leads to owned faith, but it's worth it to put in the work that goes along with accompanying them down that road. After all, you don't want them to practice the Faith just to make you happy. You want them to plant their stake in the Faith and call it their own.

On the other hand, some teens reject the Faith to put distance between themselves and their parents. While it may be unconscious, they reject the Faith as a way to reject their parents. Rarely do teens reject what the Church really teaches or what she really is. They reject what she represents in their minds. Peer-oriented teens may also reject anything their peers reject, even if their parents are loving and engaged. In these situations where the resistance or rejection is not part of the child's faith journey but rather a sign of a deeper relationship issue, we have to handle the situation delicately. We may need to deal with the attachment issue first, reengaging the teen's attachment instincts, bringing them back into the family fold and our orbit of influence. This doesn't mean the teen will immediately accept the Church, but they will at least accept our boundaries.

My second piece of advice is to set the rules and expectations about your family's faith practices upfront and as early as possible in your teen's life. Do it now if you haven't done it yet. If everyone in the family is required to participate in your family's faith life, make this rule clear. As I mentioned in a previous chapter, when they are still quite young, I tell my kids that they may eventually have doubts about God and the Church; I assure them that this is very common, and we'll get through it together. I also tell them that if they experience these doubts, they'll still attend Mass and pray with our family, because we need our community and family to make it through the deserts of doubt. So my teenagers know long before they hit the turbulence of the searching faith stage that they will still be part of our family rituals and traditions, no matter their personal opinions or questions. My teens go to Mass on Sunday because we all go; my teens pray night prayer because we all pray. I am very matter of fact about it. Our teenagers receive the graces of the sacraments and our shared prayer life even if they aren't aware of it, and God is working in their hearts if they are open to being led to the truth.

In my own mothering, I haven't yet had a teen who rejected the Church outright. Every one of my teens has doubted the Church or God at some point, but none of my teenagers has rejected the Church or God because of their doubts. If this happens someday, I will continue to require them to participate in our family's faith traditions and attend Mass with us. A teenager should still be following his parent's lead about where to go and how to live, especially if he's a young teen. If he doesn't, then I primarily have a relationship issue to address rather than a faith issue. I would work on the relationship while also sharing with my child the difference my faith makes in my life. Once a child turns eighteen, I would have to let them choose whether or not they will continue practicing their faith. I would still share with them how my faith makes my life more meaningful and my relationships better, and I would remind them of the graces of the sacraments which arm us for spiritual battle. I would still continue inviting, but I would have to respect their decision, even if

I knew they were making a mistake. We'll talk more about prodigal children in a later chapter.

A Teen's Awakening Sexuality

Teens' awakening sexuality creates some of the conflict between parents and their teens. Our hyper-sexualized culture certainly adds fuel to the fire by glamorizing casual sex and normalizing deviant sexual behavior. I remember "spin the bottle" and "truth or dare" type games when I was a teenager. Not that this was a wholesome way to spend my time, but these games are tame compared to the twisted things happening today in teen circles. A friend with a child enrolled at a local high school told me that the students regularly have oral sex parties — once at a community swimming pool behind towel barriers. Teens have been charged with felonies for broadcasting video streams of orgies. Even tweens and young teens may have a quite disturbing need to shock others with their brazen displays of skin and excessive sexual signaling.

Of course, we hope our teens will have better judgment, but we are responsible for ensuring they are not exposed to more temptation (or shocking behavior) than they can handle. A teenager's reasoning skills lag behind his sexual development, so he may behave impulsively and find himself in situations he regrets. Teens may go along with the crowd just to fly under the radar, fit in, or avoid conflict. For these reasons, parents have to be very clear about their expectations about their children's behavior on social media and in peer gatherings. While we don't want to assume the worst about our teens, we don't want to overlook signs of trouble, and we certainly don't want to court it. Teens need enough freedom to take risks as they become more independent, but they do this within established boundaries.

It's also critical that we provide them with perspective on the messages they may receive about sex in school or on social media. Introducing teens to the Church's teaching on sexuality will instill a more wholesome, integrated understanding of how their maturing sexuality fits into God's plan for them. I didn't know very much about Church teachings about sexuality, chastity, and marriage until my husband and I attended a Pre-Cana retreat when we were engaged. I think we only learned the basics, but I learned increasingly more as the years passed, especially as new resources for the laity became available. As a teenager, I knew the Church prohibited sex before marriage; I assumed the Church was saying sex is shameful. Unfortunately, many people have this same assumption. They believe the Church's teaching is repressive and unrealistic, that abstinence from extramarital sex is a form of medieval torture, and that human beings need to explore their sexuality with many partners to experience fulfillment.

First, the Church doesn't teach that sex is shameful. The Church teaches that human sexuality is a dignified gift from God, and God wants it to be a source of joy and pleasure for his children (see CCC 2362). That doesn't mean every act of sex is dignified or joyful. Like all of God's gifts, we are called to use the gift of sexuality according to its purpose in God's plan of salvation; otherwise, we deform the gift and find ourselves in pain. Pope St. John Paul II explains:

> Sexuality, by means of which man and woman give themselves to one another through the acts which are proper and exclusive to spouses, is by no means something purely biological, but concerns the innermost being of the human person as such. It is realized in a truly human way only if it is an integral part of the love by which a man and a woman commit themselves totally to one another until death. The total physical self-giving would be a lie if it were not the sign and fruit of a total

personal self-giving, in which the whole person, including the temporal dimension, is present: if the person were to withhold something or reserve the possibility of deciding otherwise in the future, by this very fact he or she would not be giving totally.[4]

While we are sexual beings even if we're unmarried, a sexual relationship is reserved for marriage between a man and woman. Sex is meant to be exclusive and integral to a relationship where both spouses give themselves to one another totally and completely. From the beginning, men and women were made to complement one another, equal in dignity but unique in how they express love for one another. An important insight from the Church that we can convey to our teens: Sexuality is not limited to sexual intercourse. Because we are a unity of body and soul, our sexuality involves not only our bodies but also our spiritual and emotional lives. According to God's design, our sexuality is a way for us to image God by giving and receiving love. If we use our sexuality in a disordered way, it hurts us and others. Using others for our sexual gratification is degrading to them and ourselves; it cuts us off from enjoying the fruits of healthy sexuality.

Purity and chastity are not signs of sexual repression or prudishness but rather a celebration and preservation of the sacred bond between spouses. Ask your teen to imagine his future spouse right now. Would he rather that she spend her time sleeping around or maturing intellectually, emotionally, and spiritually? What does he imagine his future spouse hopes for him? How can he spend his time to best prepare for that union? One of the most effective ways to raise a son or daughter who values chastity is to model chastity in our marriage. That's right: Married couples are called to be chaste. Chastity is simply the right ordering of our sexuality. Within marriage, sexuality is rightly ordered when it's open to life and self-giving rather than selfish.

Spouses are chaste when they reserve their affection and romantic attention for their spouses; it's unchaste to view pornography or even flirt with somebody outside our marriage.

Second, despite messages in movies and other media that life is more fulfilling if we have lots of sex with lots of people, liberal attitudes toward sex are correlated to a *decrease* in human well-being, not an increase. Sexually active teens are more likely to be depressed and suicidal than sexually abstinent teens, even after controlling for sex, race, age, and socioeconomic status.[5] Teens who are sexually active now are more likely to divorce and have an extramarital affair in adulthood.[6] Of course, correlation is not causation; we might identify other explanations for these outcomes. At the very least, teen sexual activity does not teach teens how to have healthy, functioning adult romantic relationships, and it impedes their social, emotional, spiritual, and even sexual development. If you've ever read some of the sexting messages between teens, you know there is something very wrong nowadays. Their sexual exploits are not indications of healthy sexuality but desperation and emptiness. Promiscuity isn't glamorous or appealing, period. The Church's teaching on sexuality reflects the truth about the human person in their totality. Our entire being is involved in our sexuality. Not just our bodies, but also our minds and our emotions. Most school-based programs miss this insight.

While not writing from a religious perspective, Dr. Gordon Neufeld says that, in many ways, traditional moral values and cultural taboos around promiscuity make sense from a developmental standpoint. He admits his views are "old-fashioned," but he says old-fashioned seems to be the most natural lifestyle for healthy sexual development. In his seminars on adolescent sexuality, he explains that teens' bodies are ready for sex long before they are emotionally ready to handle it.[7] Recall the six roots of attachment — the six ways humans can potentially hold on to and bridge separations from their attachment figures: physical proximity, sameness, belonging, significance, love (emotional intimacy), and being known (psychological intimacy). The six roots of attachment are relevant in every human relationship, including romantic relationships.

In romantic relationships, attachment becomes sexualized, and indeed healthy romantic relationships move through all six roots of attachment. Think about the beginning of your relationship with your spouse: Your relationship likely deepened as you moved more deeply into attachment, assuming you have a healthy marriage. First, you wanted to be physically near this new person in your life; perhaps you shared dinner while listening to music, which taps into the five senses. You began to discover things you had in common, and you explored those shared interests. Eventually, you sensed you belonged with your spouse and could trust him. After some time, you knew you really mattered to him — you felt special and appreciated. Eventually, you knew you could give your heart away to your spouse — you felt emotionally safe. To some extent, you felt you could share your interior world with him, which requires great vulnerability and trust.

Many schools encourage teens to practice "safe sex," but according to Neufeld, these programs fail to consider the nature of adolescent emotional development. When you consider the human heart in one's definition of safe sex, sex is safe only with people we are attached to on all six attachment levels. Even in platonic friendships, it takes a long time to reach that level of intimacy, and you reach it with very few people in a lifetime because many people are incapable of attaching at the deeper roots of attachment (significance, love, and being known). Neufeld points out, "One's sexuality can be no more developed than your capacity for relationship. If you haven't developed the capacity for attachment at the deep levels, you won't have the capacity for fully developed sexuality."[8] If we engage in sexual activity when the attachment roots are shallow or undeveloped, we are opening ourselves up to incredible wounding and heartbreak. Because he writes from a secular perspective, Neufeld doesn't say kids should wait until they're married to have sex, but he does say they should wait until they are emotionally mature enough to give their hearts away. He is concerned by the aggressiveness of teens around sex today, particularly girls, who have lost their inhibitions, often with complete strangers. In his professional view, this is not a sign of liberation but hardened hearts.[9]

Neufeld teaches that sexualized attachment has a developmental purpose: procreation and coupling.[10] These are Neufeld's terms, not mine, and they sound an awful lot like the Church's teaching that marital sexuality has two related purposes: 1) a procreative dimension in which spouses cooperate with God in giving birth to new life and 2) a unitive or relational dimension that deepens the love between spouses.[11] The Church's teaching on sexuality facilitates human flourishing and protects real love. It's just good common sense!

Parent-led sexuality education. Parents should know that many school-based sex-ed programs are inadequate and morally problematic. Kids often learn that being responsible with their sexuality merely requires that they avoid pregnancy and sexually transmitted diseases. This view leaves kids with the impression that as long as they use a condom, they are doing the right thing; they're safe. They don't learn anything about the emotional aspect of sex; they don't learn that their bodies are wired to attach to their sex partners; they don't learn that in God's plan, the sexual embrace is reserved for the marital bed. But, today's school-based sex ed programs teach kids about far more than pregnancy and disease prevention. Some schools teach teenagers to practice "safe sex" by using masturbation (both solitary and partnered), oral sex, anal penetration, and pornography. Abortion is presented as "health care." In fact, Planned Parenthood is the largest provider of sex education in public schools.[12] Know what sort of curriculum your teen's school uses for health or sex ed, and opt out if the program conflicts with your family's values.

A good sexual education program teaches not only the facts of life but also the purpose of life and how sexuality fits into that purpose. Your diocese might offer teens and their parents an alternative to the programs available in schools. For example, a diocese near me hosts an annual mother-daughter weekend where girls and their moms learn about reproduction, fertility, and the gifts of femininity. If you can't find anything similar near you, know that you have what it takes to teach your teen about healthy sexuality. The Church reminds parents that they are uniquely positioned to provide their children with an education that connects sexuality to the spiritual potential of the human person. In *The Truth and Meaning of Human Sexuality*, the Pontifical Council for the Family explains: "In view of the close links between the sexual dimension of the person and his or her ethical values, education must bring children to a knowledge of and respect for the moral norms as the necessary and highly valuable guarantee for responsible personal growth in human sexuality. *No one is capable of giving moral education in this delicate area better than duly prepared parents.*"[13] Not only do parents have a right to provide intellectual, moral, and spiritual formation to their children, but they have a heightened duty to do so when institutional programs are inadequate.[14] However, we can't help but notice the Council's mention of "duly prepared parents." What if we aren't duly prepared? What if we never learned about the Church's theology of sexuality?

Fortunately, many resources are available for parent-led, home-based sexuality formation. To build your confidence, check out Greg and Lisa Popcak's very practical *Beyond the Birds and the Bees: Raising Sexually Whole and Holy Kids*. They offer great insights and tips for raising kids with a healthy understanding of their bodies and sexuality. I also like *Raising Pure Teens* by Jason Evert and Chris Stefanick. They motivate parents with research findings on the efficacy of chastity education; they encourage parents to present the Church's teaching to teens as an appealing invitation to greatness rather than a scary warning. If you're looking for a complete curriculum to work through with your teen, I recommend the *Theology of the Body* programs published by Ascension Press, which include student and teacher guides and accompanying videos. Ascension publishes separate programs for middle schoolers and high schoolers. Their high school theology of the body program begins by discussing the nature of identity and where our identities originate, so that program would allow you to begin your sex ed discussions by clarifying how our bodies are clues to who we are as children of God.

I have some favorite resources for teens to read on their own. Jason Evert's *Theology of His Body and Theology of Her Body* is a short book divided into two parts: One half is written for teen girls and the other half for teen boys. He offers a glimpse into the nature and purpose of sexuality; teens learn that their sexuality is a gift to be protected. David Hajduk's *God's Plan for You: Life, Love, Marriage, and Sex* dives into the theological roots of the Church's teaching on human sexuality in a way that teens can understand.

Dating. My husband and I try to convey a positive message about the physical changes of puberty and our teens' interest in the opposite sex. Still, we encourage our teens to put off serious dating. Our default rule is no dating until age sixteen, but I think it's reasonable to consider each child and his or her maturity and readiness for dating. We explain to our teens the boundaries of acceptable behavior with opposite-sex friends, and we encourage group socializing with a mix of boys and girls. Before we give the nod to dating, our teens should be capable of fulfilling and healthy friendships, and they should recognize and respect the dignity of masculinity and femininity.

Teenagers may believe they are ready for serious romantic relationships long before they're actually ready. They are yearning for independence, and we can give it to them, but gradually. This is one of those situations where some conflict may be unavoidable, and our job is to hold on to our teen even while he pushes back against us. We can stand our ground, reminding our teen that we'll revisit the issue in the future, that his feelings do matter, but that we are ultimately responsible for setting the dating rules.

The teen years are better spent on self-discovery rather than serious dating. Real love requires a self-knowledge and confidence that our teens will gain with time, not premature dating. Recall that owned faith forms part of a person's identity, thoughts, and emotions ("internalized" faith), and it shapes the person's choices and actions ("externalized" faith). We want our kids to have a chance to work through the stages of faith so that they come to see themselves through the eyes of faith. Recall Pope John Paul II's teaching about "original solitude," which I introduced in a previous chapter: We must all sit in solitude before our Creator so we might come to self-knowledge and self-definition. The pope explained original solitude in his fifth general audience in 1979. In subsequent theology of the body audiences, he unpacked systematically how this solitude prepares us to recognize the gift of spousal complementarity. Our children can better understand and recognize what their beloved brings to their lives when they first understand themselves.

While my husband and I discourage serious dating, we would permit our teens to date if they were ready and interested. However, reflecting on both my own adolescence and experience as a mom, many times the teens most eager to date aren't mature enough to handle it, and some of the most mature teens I've known decide to put off dating. A teen's determination to date isn't an indication of their readiness.

Use your judgment and clarify for yourself and your teen how you'll know he or she is ready to date. Even if your teen isn't ready for dating, you can begin having fruitful conversations about it. Share your experiences with dating — what you got right and what you wish you had done differently. Share how you knew your spouse was special; what did you see in your spouse? Teach your sons how to politely ask a girl out on a date and your daughters how to accept or decline a date with charity; share good ideas for first dates and appropriate boundaries and manners. Kids aren't born knowing these things, and if they don't learn them from us, they'll absorb them from the culture. One important insight: Our marriages model for our teens how to treat their romantic partners. We should always strive to treat our spouses with regard and respect in front of our children, and when we don't, we can model how to make things right again.

If you think your teen isn't ready for the responsibility of dating, set that boundary now but be open to revisiting the issue regularly. Some parents worry that if they don't let their teenagers date, the teenagers won't know how to date later. While dating certainly helps a teen become more comfortable with social norms around dating, I wouldn't let concerns about experience determine whether or not you permit your teen to date. I wouldn't want my teens using other people to test drive their dating skills. When you think about it, the point of dating is to discern whether somebody is a potential spouse, not to practice dating so that you'll be a pro at it later when it "counts." Let's face it: Serial daters become experienced in serial break-ups; they may even become comfortable with dysfunctional relationships. Your teen might think his fourteen-year-old crush is the only girl for him, but the vast majority of teen relationships end in heartbreak. Teens can be mean after a breakup, and some of the behavior can leave life-long scars. You probably recall from your teen years that serious teen romances take on pseudo-marriage dynamics, but the "marriages" are toxic. The more two immature teens attach to one another romantically, the more jealous, controlling, and anxious they may become together. Teens who put off dating avoid a lot of drama while developing healthy friendships, exploring their interests, focusing on their studies, and deepening their faith lives.

This *free* section focused on guiding teens in developing discernment and interpersonal conflict management skills. These lessons, learned in the context of a safe attachment relationship, shape our teens' personalities and perceptions as they mature, serving them well for the rest of their lives. We shepherd our teens on this journey toward wholeness, but sometimes even shepherds can feel a bit lost. Parents go through a period of growth in discernment and interpersonal conflict management alongside their teens! We discover that God is our North Star, guiding us with his unrelenting love, revealing us to ourselves as he clarifies for us how and where to lead our teens. So often, our faith is ignited and restored through our mothering and fathering.

Reflection and Direction

- Oftentimes we believe the answer to interpersonal conflict is to change the other person, but it's more helpful to think about how we ourselves can change. How can we change our perspective, expectations, and behavior to heal the relationship? What are some ways you can change to improve your relationship with your teen?

- Think about times when your relationship with your teen seemed to be harmonious and light. What was going on during these times that might give you insights into how you can avoid conflict with your teen? For example, do you have consistent rituals and routines during these times? Do you spend more time with your teen enjoying lighthearted fun? Ask God to help you use these insights to build more godly relationships in your home.

- Reflect on your own experience with dating when you were a teen. What messages did you absorb? Do you have any regrets? How can these experiences help you guide your teen toward wholesome and holy attitudes toward the opposite sex?

Transform

Transform

7

Toward Owned Faith

Behold, I send you out as sheep in the midst of wolves;
so be wise as serpents and innocent as doves.
— MATTHEW 10:16

The Big Picture

- The marks of the end of adolescence
- Preschooler syndrome in young adults
- Recovering lost rites of passage

In this chapter, I'd like to give you a snapshot of what you might see in your teen as she approaches early adulthood. What happens ideally in terms of our teens' emotional, social, and spiritual development? What might prevent teens from launching successfully into adulthood? What might hold them back in their spiritual development?

Owned Faith and the Path of Discipleship

Previously, I explained the human capacities for attachment, emergence, and integration: These three drives energize and motivate us to move forward toward maturity, even when the movement means loss of the familiar. I mentioned that the attachment

---

What is an "adult"?

How do you know when your child reaches adulthood? Biologists might consider an adult any human who has reached sexual maturity. Developmentalists would say adults are not only physically grown-up, but they're capable of emotional control, self-sufficiency, and caring for others, so some humans never reach developmental adulthood. Other specialists consider specific milestones as signs that a child has reached adulthood; for example, moving out of the family home and becoming financially self-reliant.

In this chapter, I'm mostly using the term "adult" to refer to legal adulthood: age eighteen. This is the age of majority in nearly every state.[1] As I explain in this chapter, in reality, kids transition slowly toward mature adulthood. I'm amazed at the difference in maturity and competence in my twenty-three-year-old son compared to when he was eighteen . So, I concede in this chapter the vast difference between legal adulthood on the one hand and emotional, psychological, social, and spiritual maturity on the other.

---

and emergence drives are dominant in our children and teens: Our kids are primarily working on getting their bearings in their primary relationships (attachment) and figuring out their identity and their purpose in the world (emergence).

Think about how faith development plays out during these early years. Our kids' faith lives tend to mirror our own: They go where we go and tend to believe what we believe. Then, as they begin to feel the rumblings and excitement of adolescence, they may enter the searching faith stage. The wrestling in the searching faith stage is part of the emergent process. While our teens should continue participating in our family's faith practices, we can support their increasing capacity to take responsibility for their own faith lives. They need permission to confront their doubts and questions even if they make us nervous; they need room to explore different prayer approaches and devotional practices even if we aren't drawn to those particular approaches and practices. Our teens do not need to reject the Church or our faith traditions as they mature. However, they do need to face their doubts and questions about the Church with an open mind and heart.

Toward the end of the teen years, we may notice many lights turn on for our kids. If they are securely attached to safe adults, they will blossom into independent, confident young adults with a coherent sense of self. Their personalities will be robust; they will know where they leave off and others begin; they will possess strong boundaries in their relationships and expect to be treated well by others. These young people have the capacity for integrative functioning: They can mix with peers without blending into them; they can participate in a community without being absorbed by it. They can live inside their own skin and stand on their own feet while respecting the right of others to do the same. They lose the impulsiveness and egocentrism of childhood. The capacity for integration appears in flashes in later childhood and adolescence; however, because integration requires emotional and cognitive maturity, our kids will not be fully capable of integration until the later teen years or early adulthood. Even then, they will continue to work on integration for the rest of their lives as they come to understand themselves in relation to others and to God, and as they come to accept and respect the personhood and dignity of others around them.

Toward the end of adolescence, we may also see evidence that our teens are taking greater ownership of their faith lives and spiritual growth. Making the Faith their own doesn't mean they take on a hyper-personalized, made-up spirituality, but we want them to choose God as he chooses them, and we want them to seek clarity about how they are personally called to serve God and his Church. Owned faith is marked by a transformation of identity and purpose. After the struggles of doubting in the stage before it, owned faith often feels like blinders have been removed from our eyes. This illumination may occur suddenly during a homily or while reading a book, or it may take many years of study, prayer, and exploring. What is distinct about this stage of faith is that the believer's interior self-perception and exterior actions change in response to their faith in God. Their faith is *internalized* in how they think and feel, and it is *externalized* in the choices they make.

When our children enter the owned faith stage, they embark on the discipleship path. In the first century, discipleship was marked by *imitation*. The disciple didn't learn only what the rabbi thought, but followed his way of life as well. As Catholic theologian Edward Sri clarifies, the goal was "to imitate the way he lived: the way he prayed, studied, taught, served the poor, and lived out his relationship with God day-to-day."[2] It's the same for disciples today: We seek to imitate Christ in how we pray, give, and live. As we follow him and experience a sense of belonging with him, our identities are transformed as we come to see ourselves the way Christ sees us, to know ourselves the way Christ knows us.

Imitating, following, belonging, being known. Does this sound familiar? Discipleship is nothing less than an attachment relationship. As I explore in my first book, we are our children's first teachers, and they are our disciples. Healthy, securely attached children imitate their parents; they want to be like their parents and look to them as a model for how to be in the world. God wired our kids this way so that we can keep them safe and lead them where they should go. But ultimately, we want our children to turn their gaze toward Christ; we want our children to yearn to be like Jesus and to look to him as their model for how to think, work, and love in the world.

Emergence and owned faith are surely connected, but not all emergent kids have reached the owned faith stage. We hope our children become thriving adults with healthy interpersonal relationships and rich faith life. But, while some teens transition quickly into the owned faith stage, others will remain in the searching faith stage well into adulthood, even if they are emergent and show a capacity for healthy social integration. Your teen may grapple with doubts and distractions well into adulthood. Hopefully, she will continue to frequent the sacraments and find comfort in the familiarity of the Church's liturgical celebrations and devotionals; if she is faithful, she will find her way. Unfortunately, some teens may resist God's lead, not necessarily because their parents did something wrong in raising them, but because they're human and vulnerable to the snares of Satan. I have known on-fire Catholic parents who were intentional in their parenting, prioritizing faith in their homes, yet their kids fell away from the Church. In the next chapter, I'll talk about what you can do in such circumstances.

Crossing the Bridge to Adulthood

Adolescence is a bridge between childhood and adulthood. On the journey over that bridge, we want our kids to move from complete dependence on us toward confident independence, but we don't want them to stop there. Ultimately, we want them to be mature enough for interdependence in a loving community of faith and perhaps their own families, if that is their vocational calling. The purpose — the end — of adolescent development isn't to lead the child toward radical autonomy but rather integration into a community of believers living out the call of discipleship together.

We also want our kids to move from mimicking and mirroring our faith toward a sense of personal commitment to a God who loves them and guides them. The purpose of human development isn't to lead the child toward radical separation, but rather attachment to God, the source of our being, the perfect answer to all our longings. Indeed, the drive within us to take our place in a family, community, and society is a sign of our longing for the original grace of perfect harmony with God and others before the Fall. In this life, we are capable of growing continually in virtue so that we become increasingly free to give and receive love.[3]

This bridge between childhood and adulthood sometimes feels wobbly. There are many dark moments, setbacks, outbursts, and regrets (for both teens and their parents). In reality, our kids have the drives within them to navigate the bridge, but sometimes they need cheerleaders, reality checkers, and maybe the end of a shepherd's staff pushing them along! This period is hard for parents because it's often so hard for teenagers. I've come to appreciate how scary growing up is for my teenagers. They are letting go of their childhoods and facing the uncertainties of adulthood. While growing up is exciting, it's also terrifying. When our teens are anxious or moody, often our impulse is to fix the problem, but usually, the emotional turmoil of the teen years begins to calm naturally. They certainly need reminders, guidance, and encouragement, but often, the best thing we can do is hold on to our teens so they don't fall over the edge of the developmental bridge.

Toward the end of adolescence, you'll probably notice your teen becoming soft again, or at least more even-tempered. This settling is a natural result of our teens' maturing brains and increasing emotional control, but it's also a sign that they see the light of childhood dimming. They begin talking about their favorite childhood movies, memories of family vacations, and their favorite Sunday meals. They know their departure from the familiarity and safety of home is looming, and they want to hold on a little longer. In fact, they want both to leave home and hold on to it at the same time. These mixed feelings are natural and a quintessential mark of the ending of childhood. In the sadness is anticipation; as the door of childhood closes, the gate of adulthood opens wide.

Failure to Launch

In the last chapter, I mentioned the conflict triggered between parents and their teens when teens fail to follow through on their chores, homework, and similar commitments. Most of the time, our teens simply need reminders and guidance while learning to accept responsibility for their obligations and manage their calendars. They mess up, but typically, they learn from their mistakes as the years pass. By the end of the teen years, though, they should have this issue under control (for the most part).

If your young adult child still fails to show up for appointments or forgets to register for his college classes, or if he seems to start then quickly lose interest in potential careers, he may be stuck in immaturity. This is what social scientists call failure to launch syndrome; Dr. Gordon Neufeld calls it "preschooler syndrome."[4] It's not unusual for a preschooler to beg to take karate, then want to drop it after one lesson, but if an eighteen-year-old does the same thing, particularly if he does this continually, it may be a sign that he lacks emergent energy and integrative functioning. Dr. Neufeld remarks, "Many adults have not attained maturity — have not mastered being independent, self-motivated individuals capable of tending their own emotional needs and of respecting the needs of others."[5] As I noted earlier in this book, teens all grow up physically, but many fail to grow up emotionally and psychologically. They may flunk adolescence partly because they resist the realities and responsibilities of adulthood. Mature young adults work hard, set and keep goals, and meet the expectations set by teachers and employers. They can see the rewards or the good to come down the road even when they're uncomfortable in the moment; with that insight, they temper their impulse to give up or take the easy way out. Mature young adults have grit. In contrast, immature young adults seem to lack direction or long-term goals. They can't hold down jobs or finish academic programs because they can't delay gratification or tolerate the discomfort of hard work.

Evidently, failure to launch syndrome is far more common in boys than girls.[6] In his compelling book *Leaving Boyhood Behind*, Catholic dad Jason Craig describes men who continue living as if they are boys: "They avoid setting out on their own. They forgo marriage and instead choose to live with their parents, play video games, and look at pornography for much of the day."[7] Craig argues that modern society delays maturity for men because it continues treating them like boys or even punishes young men for doing manly things. Boys are often ready for difficult challenges, but they are discouraged from doing anything too rambunctious or dangerous.[8] Craig's book does a marvelous job of unpacking the problem and offering solutions, including men taking the lead in teaching boys how to grow up.

Dr. Neufeld believes peer orientation is the "main culprit" for the problem of failure to launch. "Immaturity and peer orientation go hand in hand. The earlier the onset of peer orientation in a child's life and the more intense the preoccupation with peers, the greater the likelihood of being destined to perpetual childishness."[9] Teens become like their attachment figures, so if they are primarily attached to their peers, they will remain immature like their peers. This has tremendous implications for faith development. Most teenagers in our parishes are in the affiliative faith stage where they want to feel they belong. They seek validation and spiritual guidance from their attachment figures in their parishes. They're willing to go where their shepherds lead them. If a fifteen-year-old's primary attachment figure at church is another fifteen-year-old, he'll possibly stall out in the affiliative faith stage. He may never ask the hard questions associated with the searching faith stage because he will fixate on needing to fit in with the peer. Hopefully, our teens have a few friends who are spiritually vibrant, but these friends cannot provide the same inspiration, nurturing, and experience as adult guides.

When young adults move into the owned faith stage, they incorporate what they gained in the previous faith stages. They can't skip over those early stages. They need a continued sense of belonging and love from their attachment village at church (affiliative) and a clarified knowledge about the content of their faith (searching). They take their hearts and their heads with them into discipleship. If they avoid the work of the early stages, they will never reap the rewards of discipleship.

Dr. Neufeld and Jason Craig are both correct: The crisis of maturity in Western society is rooted in peer orientation and a lack of strong alpha leadership. These are problems of attachment. The natural drives to grow up work only within safe and secure hierarchical attachments — they work only when adults lead the young. If those attachments are absent or weak, the teen will struggle to mature. Additionally, teens can be locked in immaturity because of their own fears, even when parents and other adults in their lives provide consistent and warm guidance in how to become an adult. Recall the void of adolescence, which our teens must fill with their growing awareness of their unique identity and purpose as children of God. This void creates a crisis that every teen needs the courage to confront. Some teens may try to fill the void with a false self that is constructed from lies they absorb from culture or friends. Or they may resist facing the fears and sadness that accompany the loss of childhood. If they fail to navigate the void of adolescence, they will fail to grow up emotionally, socially, and spiritually.

God's Backup Plan

The good news is that when the natural human drives to grow up don't work, God has a backup plan. Our family's cultural roots and faith traditions provide a structure for young people as they wrestle through the attachment void. These practices keep our teens connected to the communities that can sustain them through the uncertainties of adolescent development. When the natural drives within our kids need a little boost, our cultural practices can help out. In particular, coming-of-age rites and traditions can carry kids forward even when they lack enough emergent energy to do the work of maturing.[10] When the pull of emergence doesn't work, the push of culture can.

Anthropologist Arnold van Gennep studied such rites of passage in different cultures in different periods of history, and he believed they are a natural impulse in all human communities. He identified three distinct stages in the passage from child to adult:[11]

- **Separation:** preparing for and marking the necessary separations of growing up

- **Initiation or Transition:** sharing rituals of transition in which the young person is guided by adults in understanding what it means to be a man or a woman
- **Incorporation:** returning to the community with one's identity clarified; taking one's place alongside adults

Van Gennep saw these stages in nearly every society he studied. Culture can provide the means through which young people confront the losses of growing up; it can offer them something they want more than what is lost; namely, the honor of adult status. Cultural rituals can help teens understand and yearn for adulthood: they know what adulthood looks like, they want it, and they have mentors to get them there. For instance, during the Age of the Samurai, in a ritual called *genpuku,* Japanese adolescents received their first Samurai armor, including a helmet to replace the fabric caps that Japanese boys wore. Similarly, at about age twelve, aboriginal Australian boys were sent into the wilderness alone on a journey of self-discovery and spiritual transformation. In these cultures, adults led the youth to face the void of adolescence and fill it with a vision of themselves as an adult. These rites of passage provided a catalyst for adolescents' sense of pride in growing up; they prized the marks of honor that accompanied these experiences. Most significantly, these rites determined their destiny, at least in early adulthood.

Let me share one modern rite of passage from a sub-culture in the United States. Catholic girls with Latin American roots often have a *quinceañera* to celebrate their fifteenth birthdays.[12] These elaborate celebrations include a Mass and unique traditions that initiate the girl into womanhood. For example, the girl's father removes her flat shoes and replaces them with high heels. (This reminds me of my Great-Aunt Irene's story, which

I shared in chapter one, about the day she was allowed to wear "lady shoes.") She throws a "quince" doll to the younger girls, indicating she's leaving dolls behind. She wears a ball gown and performs a formal dance with a "court" of fifteen young men and fourteen young women (so fifteen couples) who prepare for months to perform their dance together. In traditional Mexican culture, girls weren't allowed to dance with non-family males until they were fifteen, so this dance signals her entry into the world of dating. These traditions provide many things lacking in most modern homes: a sense of ritual, a link to the young lady's heritage, and a recognition that she's moving toward adulthood. And we can see that the *quinceañera* has all the hallmarks of an effective rite of passage. There is a time of preparation, lessons to be learned, a ritual to mark the transition, and adults receiving the young person into more grown-up relationships. After their *quinceañera*, the teenagers are no longer viewed as little girls, and they are expected to leave childhood behind moving forward.

Rites of passage like these help teens reach for adulthood even when they have some kind of emotional or attachment issue holding them back. Van Gennep's model might help us correct or avoid preschooler syndrome in our youth. While we don't need to adopt the specific rites of other societies, we can draw on them for inspiration. We can contemplate van Gennep's stages as Catholic Christians who have a specific understanding of the purpose of human life.

Separation, Preparation, and Reunion

Van Gennep's discussion of separation fascinates me because of what I learned about separation in Dr. Neufeld's work. Dr. Neufeld believes that we need to understand and manage separation in our children's lives if they are going to reach their developmental potential. Recall that separation is the fundamental human fear.[13] In an emergency, we don't immediately look for food and shelter; we look for our people. Fixing and avoiding separation preoccupies our hearts and minds. However, from the moment we are born until we die, our lives are filled with many unavoidable separations. Our first steps away from Mommy, our first day of school, moving away from home, or a grandparent dying: Each of these life events involves separating ourselves from the people we love and the roles we played in their lives. Separating from childhood and our parents are two such inevitable losses that our teens must accept if they're going to grow up and take their place in the world.

In a coming-of-age rite of passage, the separation doesn't necessarily involve a drastic physical separation as it did for the twelve-year-old aboriginal boy who went off alone into the wilderness to survive with the animals (which today would likely end in a visit from child protective services). The separation may take the form of the parent entrusting the child to another adult who mentors the child. All coming-of-age rituals also share in common a time of preparation for the transition stage toward adulthood, and an adult, never another child, leads the child in this preparation. In fact, devoted adult mentorship is one of the notable features in the coming-of-age rites that van Gennep studied: A trusted adult teaches the young person how to dress, talk, and behave like an adult. In religious communities, wise adults give the youth lessons about the beliefs and practices of their religious tradition. Girls are nearly always taught by women and boys by men. An important clarification: In coming-of-age rites of passage, the point of the separation isn't to destroy a child's relationships with his family of origin; it is to turn the child into an adult who successfully reintegrates into the community with a sense of purpose and a clarified identity. The separation leads to growth and reunion.

Family life is filled with opportunities for recovering the essence of these rituals as our kids grow up. When your child first goes to school or a sleep-away camp, these are separations that show your child is growing up. Small separations become bigger separations in the teen years, often involving intense preparation: leveling up in scouts, attaining a driver's license, applying for a first job, or choosing a college. These seemingly ordinary moments can include a sense of ritual and mentorship. We can invite members of our teen's attachment village who are willing to share their experience, tips, and excitement with the teen as the event approaches (whether it is the scouting promotion, the driving test, finishing college applications, etc.). Then, after the event, we mark the moment with a celebration of our teen's emerging independence, competence, and responsibility.

Such rituals mark the course for a child as he moves toward adulthood. He knows he doesn't have to figure out on his own what it means to be an adult. He feels supported as he faces increasing challenges, receives words of wisdom from people who love him, and knows those same people will be there for him as he ventures forward well into adulthood.

A Word about Bridging Separations

Small and big separations may be painful in the transition to adulthood. If your child is scared or hesitant, try bridging the separation. When we bridge, we point our child to the next point of connection so that she can more readily accept the separation and adjust. We do this intuitively with young children: "I can't wait to see you after school at 3:00! Let's go out for ice cream." By focusing on the next point of contact rather than pushing her face into the separation, you ease your child into the separation, helping her hold on to you until you connect again. We can continue to bridge with older kids and teenagers through their own difficult separations.

Let me share an example. When my older son was a freshman in high school, I drove him several hours away to attend a week-long boot camp for the Civil Air Patrol. Cadets were not permitted to phone their parents during the week. On the drive down, my son expressed concern about what he was taking on. He wasn't sure he could handle it. He imagined the rigor, the yelling, the expectations; he was fearful about facing these challenges without the support of his parents. I encouraged him on that drive down, but as we leaned down in our car trunk to pull out his bags, he whispered, "Don't leave me here." Now there are some situations in which the answer here would be to back off. We should not launch too early or force separation before a child is emotionally ready. However, sometimes it's hard to know whether the child is just having natural jitters or we are pushing too early. In this situation, I sensed that my son was ready, that he just needed a nudge forward. He had wanted to go only a few days before, and he was showing signs of needing a challenge away from home, so I did in the moment what I thought was best. I bridged the separation to make it more manageable for him. I told him I would be in town overnight and that if something happened before the next day, I would be nearby. I told him I would be praying for him every day, checking the Civil Air Patrol website for pictures and stories about what he was up to, and that in a week, I would be in the stands when he graduated. Sometimes, I am not absolutely confident about my decisions in my mothering, and this was such a time.

I wondered all week whether or not I had made a mistake. I did check the website and saw a few images of my son — all his limbs seemed to be attached, and he was working hard; that was about all I could detect. When I arrived to pick him up a week later, I was indeed in the stands. I watched him march with his unit and graduate. Then the parents were escorted to an auditorium to watch a slideshow of the week while the cadets remained with their units in the same auditorium. Though I could see him, I had not been able to talk to my son at all. Finally, when the presentation ended, the cadets were released, and I was able to hug my son and talk to him. He told me he had had so much fun that he didn't want to leave! He'd had a challenging week, but he faced his fears and grew in leadership and confidence. We stopped for lunch on the way home; I told him how proud I was of him, that he showed great courage and grit by facing his fears and tackling the challenge. As an extra bonus, he now knows how to fold T-shirts into itty-bitty tubes and make his bed with razor-sharp precision.

I've described adolescence as a "bridge" between childhood and adulthood, and in this section I'm using the term bridge again to describe this intuitive way that parents help their kids survive separations. Well, we can bridge the bridge of adolescence! We can remind our teens that even when they are adults, they will still be our kids, and we'll still be their moms and dads. Their growing up will not change how much we love them, and we will continue being a safe harbor for them anytime they need a place to rest.

Confirmation: The Sacrament of Mission

When I began this discussion about coming-of-age rites of passage, you may have immediately thought about the Sacrament of Confirmation. While confirmation is certainly a rite of passage, it isn't meant to be a *coming-of-age* rite of passage like the *quinceañera*. Confirmation is not a sign of *physical* maturing but rather *sacramental* maturing. Confirmation may happen at many different points in the child's life, not necessarily in the teen years. Indeed, children were once confirmed in early childhood on the same day — or years before — they received their First Communion.[14] In the Eastern and Orthodox churches, children are still confirmed in infancy, and some Roman Catholic dioceses have returned to this order of the sacraments. As a sign of sacramental maturing, confirmation is the transmission of identity and mission, not a signal that the child is all grown up.

Of course, if your child is confirmed in high school, the sacrament probably does feel like a transition to adulthood like a
coming-of-age rite of passage. You can view the confirmation
process this way, but ensure your teen understands confirmation
with the heart and mind of the Church. I think the focus should
be on spiritual and intellectual transformation rather than physical transformation, but, given that lots of physical changes may
be happening at the same time in your house, you can be creative! Along with some suggestions I offer here for leading your
teen spiritually and intellectually through confirmation, you
can incorporate practical lessons in what it means to become
an adult.

The Confirmation Cliff

In researching modern cultural rites of passage for this chapter, I
learned more about the Jewish bar and bat mitzvah, the entrance
of young Jewish boys and girls into adult Jewish society. Ideally,
under the guidance of adult leaders, the young person studies
the Torah, learns to recite Jewish prayers, takes on a mitzvah
project, and learns social etiquette. Young Jewish boys receive
the "tefillin" — the black leather boxes containing Jewish scripture. Girls often have female mentors who guide them in what
it means to be a Jewish woman. Ideally, the mitzvah becomes a
stepping stone into full participation in Jewish life, where the
young people are expected to take on responsibilities in their
communities. You can see how the mitzvah has all the marks of
an effective rite of passage. However, many Jewish youths and
even their parents increasingly view the mitzvah as the end of
religious training and all obligations to their Jewish community
(including their parents).[15]

We have this same issue with confirmation in the Church.
Many confirmands assume they are graduating from church

when they're confirmed! They think their time of "doing religion" is over. Confirmation is a rite of passage, indeed, but the passage isn't an exit door! It is a door that opens to a mission. As intentional Catholic parents, we can be mindful of our conversations about confirmation in our homes. Parents can become too fixated on details of the party that follows the confirmation Mass (the cake, the color of the napkins, the music) that it signals to the confirmand that the day is about a party. Undoubtedly, the celebration is an important aspect of marking the moment, but in our conversations at home, perhaps we can focus more on the dignity and blessings of the sacrament than on the party.

What are these blessings? Why does confirmation matter? Through the graces of the sacrament, the confirmand becomes united more firmly to Christ, with an increase in the gifts of the Holy Spirit and special strength to spread and defend the Faith (see CCC 1303). This isn't a substitute Holy Spirit filling in while the real Holy Spirit is off doing more important things! Our teens receive the same outpouring of the Holy Spirit that the apostles received on Pentecost. They are empowered for their mission of transforming the culture for Christ, in whatever form that may take as the years unfold. This doesn't mean they will be filled with a Ph.D. in theology, but they will be filled with the Holy Spirit, who will guide them in where to go and what to say as they live as friends of Jesus Christ.

As intentional Catholic parents, we can be mindful of our role in supporting and leading our teens through confirmation. Your parish probably has a decent confirmation program — most of them provide something but rarely everything that a teen needs to be truly prepared for the sacrament. So you can supplement with your own leadership and faith practices at home. Like all rites of passage, our home-based confirmation prep should involve a few important elements: adult mentorship, meaningful challenges, and a clarifying of the teen's identity.

Adult Mentorship

In an earlier chapter, I emphasized the power of parents in successful faith transmission to children. As an alternative to huge youth groups, I also recommended micro-ministry teams where adults lead a handful of teenagers. Such adult guidance is particularly necessary during confirmation preparation. Our teens need adults who will help them understand the significance of the sacrament and who will inspire them to take it all seriously. They need adults in their lives who are willing to show them the way of mature faith, and they need those adults to stick with them long after the confirmation party is over. At the very least, we can help our teens choose a confirmation sponsor who will take them under their wing and who is serious about his or her faith. Without engaged, consistent adult leadership, we lose teens after confirmation. Just as teens don't graduate from church after confirmation, adults don't graduate from being the spiritual leaders in these kids' lives! Teens need continued guidance, support, and encouragement as they enter young adulthood.

Meaningful Challenges

This is important. All rites of passage involve an "ordeal" of some kind, which is meant to strengthen the young person and pluck him out of his self-centeredness. Confirmands need spiritual, intellectual, and service challenges. God wants them to use their heads, hearts, and hands as they take up their missions, so they need challenges that help them deepen their understanding of these gifts. We can accompany our teens on some of these challenges or find other adults to guide them (the confirmation sponsor is one obvious choice), but such challenges are commonly lacking in confirmation programs. Perhaps leaders assume we'll lose the teens if we make it too hard, but we may lose them anyway if we don't challenge them.

Our teens' spiritual habits now will carry over into their young adulthoods, so confirmation is a good time for them to get serious about their spiritual lives. Do they have a prayer life? Can they count on God in a crisis? Do they feel cherished by God? Only by moving toward God will they realize how close God has been to them all along. So, begin a conversation about the importance of good spiritual habits. Good habits of any kind create grooves in the road of our lives; they help us do the right thing without thinking about it. Our character is formed and forged by these habits. If your teen has a regular habit of prayer during non-stressful times, she's deepening her friendship with God so that she will more naturally turn to him in a crisis. Challenge your teen to stretch herself spiritually by making specific prayer and devotional commitments. She might commit to praying the Rosary daily, spending Friday at 3:00 p.m. in adoration at your parish, or trying a new devotion. She can change this commitment seasonally. Make a formal written spiritual plan to help the teen persevere when she's tempted to skip her devotions. She might also have a prayer partner, such as the confirmation sponsor or relative.

Challenge your teen to stretch herself intellectually by studying her Catholic Faith more seriously. If your parish's confirmation program is heavy on games and light on content, supplement with some home-based catechetical and apologetics training. Teenagers can handle more rigorous and complex theology than we give them credit for. If you're looking for a complete program, Ascension Press's *Chosen* confirmation program is affordable and easy for parents to use at home with their teens. Otherwise, just choose some topics that you want to explore with your teen. Can she answer basic questions about the Catholic Faith? What is the Magisterium? Why do we have a pope? A straightforward resource is *100 Things Every Catholic Teen Should Know* from Life Teen. The book provides answers to one hundred questions about the Catholic Faith. One summer, I read it aloud during our family's lunchtime faith reading; it took no more than five minutes a day.

When my older son was preparing for confirmation, he became interested in the signs used in the Confirmation rite (see CCC 1293–1301). He studied these signs and prepared a presentation to deliver to his peers in his confirmation program. As he discovered, the signs of confirmation bestow great dignity on the confirmand:

- **The Anointing:** Anointing with oil on the forehead has roots in Judaism. In the Old Testament, three types of people were anointed: priests, prophets, and kings. These three roles are the three offices that we receive as baptized Christians. We share in a common priesthood, united in Christ, sacrificing ourselves for the good of others as Christ sacrificed himself for all humankind (see CCC 901–903). As prophets, we seek and teach the truth (CCC 904–907), and as kings (or queens!), we lead through self-governance and a pursuit of virtue, thereby infusing "culture and human works with a moral value" (CCC 908–910). So, remind your teen that she is a priest, a prophet, and a queen! She received the call to these offices at baptism, but the call will be clarified and deepened at confirmation.
- **The Laying On of Hands:** The laying on of hands at baptism and confirmation was present in early Church doctrine. This ritual "perpetuates the grace of Pentecost in the Church" (CCC 1288), infusing the soul with the gifts of the Holy Spirit. These gifts aid your teen in doing through Christ's power what she couldn't possibly do by her own power. With the power of the Holy Spirit, she can speak the truth in the face of disapproval or even punishment; she can

> love the undesirable and the lost.
>
> • **The Seal of the Holy Spirit:** At the time of anointing, the bishop proclaims, "Be sealed with the Holy Spirit." The words effect a change in the confirmand; his soul receives the indelible seal of Christ (CCC 1304). In ancient times, a soldier was marked with his leader's seal. Similarly, when confirmed, your teen bears Christ's seal, which shows that she belongs to Christ and is enrolled as a soldier in his army. Your teen becomes a spiritual warrior!

After witnessing my son's appreciation for these signs, I prioritize teaching them to my other children and CCD students. Some parents and youth believe confirmation is about the confirmand confirming that they accept the Faith they received at baptism, but this is a misunderstanding. The Church confirms that the young person is ready to receive the fullness of the Holy Spirit and the completion of what was begun in baptism. The Church, through the rite (the signs and rituals) of confirmation, confers the graces they need to grow into their spiritual combat boots. The anointing, laying on of hands, and the seal signify life-altering realities: The confirmand receives real graces as she journeys toward holiness; she receives a real promise of Christ's protection as the confirmand lives out in a fallen world the triple offices of priest, prophet, and king or queen. This is all much more mind-blowing than the size of the confirmation cake or the color of the napkins!

Many religious rites of passage challenge the young person with some sort of community service project. This is particularly important for Catholic confirmands because confirmation is a sacrament of self-sacrifice: Through confirmation, we receive the gifts that we need to serve others and bring them the message of Christ's mercy and healing love.[16] If your parish doesn't incorporate service into the confirmation preparation process, you can help your teen brainstorm her own project, preferably with her sponsor. She can even invite some other confirmands and their sponsors to join her. She might serve on a ministry team at church, wash dishes for your parish fish fry during Lent, help a sibling with homework once a week, or plan and build a new bench for a grandparent's garden. Whatever it is, the confirmation service project should stretch a teen outside her comfort zone. Offering themselves in service during their confirmation preparation should not be optional for confirmands; it challenges them to move beyond themselves and to begin taking the steps toward mature faith by sharing their gifts and blessings with others.

Clarified Identity and Mission

Confirmation also provides us another opportunity to guide our teens in clarifying their identities and how this identity is related to their mission and vocation in life. I've touched on this topic several times throughout our time together, but it's worth repeating. Looming over every teen are basic questions about who they are and what they should do with their lives. However, popular culture and even social science give teens the message that the answers to all their questions about life and themselves are inside of themselves — that if they just think about it hard enough, they will understand themselves and figure out how to "be authentic." Unfortunately, being authentic seems to have something to do with making yourself up as you go along, and if anybody (especially parents and other grown-ups) challenges your self-construction, they are preventing your flourishing. This is the navel-gazing approach to self-discovery, which leads to self-obsession and perhaps knowledge of one's navel, but never wisdom and self-knowledge.

Without a consideration of the order of the created world, including human nature, we tend to flop around like fish out of water. We live with tension, contradiction, and pain instead of inner peace and contentment. Human existence has a source and a purpose, and you can't understand the purpose without going to the source. Our teens will understand themselves and their purpose only when they come to understand their Creator. Here's the thing: Our teens don't have all the answers inside of themselves, but they do have the questions implanted in their natures. In *Fides et Ratio*, Pope John Paul II states confidently, "God has placed in the human heart a desire to know the truth — in a word, to know himself — so that, by knowing and loving God, men and women may also come to the fullness of truth about themselves." Paradoxically, the more we move our focus from ourselves toward God and others, the more we become ourselves and come to understand ourselves. Furthermore, only through surrendering ourselves to the divine will can we fulfill our potential. Our ideas and vision are limited, but when we unite ourselves to Christ, when we pursue holiness and the will of God, we become empowered to go places and do things we could never do before. (Theologians have a fancy word for this: *theosis*.) So, during confirmation, we have an opportunity to keep our teens grounded in truth and reality. We can remind our teenagers that the more holy they become and the more they understand God, the more they will understand themselves.

Confirmation may be a good time to begin talking to your teen more intentionally about vocational discernment. I touched on this topic in an earlier chapter. Hopefully, family conversations and family prayer include questions and curiosity about the vocational callings for all the children in the household. This is particularly important if your teen is preparing for confirmation as an older teen who will launch off into the world in a few years. As he approaches adulthood, your teen will hear a lot of advice about getting into a great college and getting a good job, but you can remind him that the top rung on the ladder is heaven, not Harvard or a CEO's chair. So, while we can certainly help our teens identify their passions and where those passions might lead them in terms of a career, we can also help them think about what clues those passions and talents might give to their "big call" in life. In particular, if we never raise with our teens the possibility that they could be called to religious life (both boys and girls) or the priesthood (boys), it won't be on their radars. Bring your confirmand to a few religious houses in your area; invite religious brothers and sisters and priests to your home. Make it normal to think and talk about becoming a religious or a priest.

Young adults can feel frustrated not knowing what God's plan is for them, particularly their state of life calling. God may ask them to wear many hats before they figure out what the big call really is. As I said in an earlier chapter, if they focus on being faithful and loving in their current relationships, if they deepen their prayer lives and their love for God, if they frequent the sacraments, they are going where they need to go and becoming the man or woman God is calling them to be. Vocational discernment often feels like we're walking through a cloud. We cannot see the endpoint; we only know what we're meant to do today, but no more than this. That is part of trusting God, knowing he will reveal what we need to know when we need to know it. Sometimes a young adult may be preparing to enter a particular career field, but through prayer and self-honesty, he realizes he does not feel a deep sense of satisfaction and peace with this plan. It might look good on paper, but it doesn't give him joy or lasting happiness. This may be a clue that he needs to turn in a different direction or at least investigate the possibility. It doesn't mean that his education was a waste. Indeed, God may have wanted him in that particular educational program as background for a reason he doesn't recognize yet.

Discipleship isn't a single moment but a long transformation of deepening self-understanding and intensifying love for Christ. It is marked by growth in holiness as the disciple grows in wisdom, but also setbacks as the disciple wrestles with his inclinations toward sin and Satan's determination to derail him. If your child becomes a disciple, he will recognize two fundamental truths: the truth about himself and the truth about what he's made for.[17] He knows he's made for heaven and for greatness, but he can be honest with himself about his weaknesses and failures. Remember that as we move on to new stages of faith, we don't leave behind the previous stages. Entering the stage of owned faith and discipleship living does not mean we have come to the end of our doubts and faith struggles, but these struggles do seem to have a different intensity and we have more resources to draw upon to find answers. Discipleship doesn't mean we no longer look to others as examples and models, but Christ does become our great model. Wherever your teen is in her spiritual path, continue praying for her and trusting in God's guidance.

Reflection and Direction

- Do you recall any special rituals or traditions in your childhood that marked specific milestones in your maturing? How did these rituals make you feel? How might you adapt these in your own home?
- Identify five coming-of-age moments that your teen will experience in the next few years. Are there adults who can participate in the preparatory stage of these important events? Could Grandpa help with driving lessons? Could a favorite uncle help study for college entrance exams? How can you mark these moments with recognition and celebration?

8
Your Faith Journey: Gaining Perspective

Acquire the spirit of peace, and thousands around you will be saved.

— St. Seraphim of Sarov

The Big Picture

- Making God your safe harbor during parenting storms
- Letting go of what isn't yours to hold
- Evangelizing your teen through your own faith life

I've shared many ideas about how you can get in the lead with your teen so you can shepherd her toward maturity. As a kind of cheerleader and big sister, I've been urging you to become what you are: the answer to your teen's emotional needs and her first spiritual director. In this chapter, I would like to shift my focus from your teen to you. The parenting vocation brings great joy and satisfaction, but it can also bring pain, frustration, and loss. How do you navigate these struggles, and what do they have to teach us?

Leaning on God

One of the most challenging lessons I had to learn as a mother is that I'm responsible for my children, but I'm not in control of outcomes. Some things are our job as parents and others aren't; some things we can change and others are beyond our control. When our relationships are rightly ordered, when we place God first in our lives, we learn to let go of what is not ours to hold. In fact, God wants to hold some things for us — things that are too hot or prickly for us to manage. As somebody with anxious attachment, I tend to hold on to everything. I try to micromanage circumstances, people, and outcomes. On some level, I believe that if I work hard enough, everything will turn out okay in the end. I fret and control because it makes me feel safer in some way, but it's really an illusion. Instead of making circumstances and relationships safer or better, I end up making myself and others miserable. Worse, as my children watch me managing my life (and everyone else's), I am not modeling surrender to and trust in God.

I will probably struggle with this tendency for longer than I care to admit. Still, I do think that by strengthening my relationship with God, by nurturing my attachment to him, I've been able to trust him more and more. My sense of security once depended on the approval of others, which left my sense of well-being under constant threat because such approval is so precarious. Now I see myself more realistically, in the context of my purpose and identity as a daughter of God. I am so flawed and small, yet I am loved and treasured by my heavenly Father. I don't recognize this only intellectually; I have absorbed this reality in my soul, and it reflects in the way I relate to others and how I expect others to relate to me. This shift in my perceptions and personality happened only through God's grace as he met me in prayer and the sacraments. "I am here," he said. "Come and sit with me a while. Let me hold that mask for you."

The most important way parents can prepare for and survive the trials of parenting is to nourish our relationship with God through prayer, devotional practices, and frequenting the sacraments. God has helped me breathe again when I thought I was suffocating; he has been the lighthouse in a sea of losses. An important insight from spiritual directors: A crisis is not the best time to learn to discern God's presence or develop new prayer habits. So often, we ignore God until we're in a pickle, then we throw out a prayer like we insert a quarter in a candy machine. Imagine if your spouse never talked to you unless he needed something from you. It would be a sign of a lack of love, and he would never really know you. That's what we're missing when we use God like a candy machine: We're missing the most fundamental and fulfilling of relationships. Building a solid relationship with God in calm times will help us lean on him more comfortably and naturally through the parenting storms.

Give yourself the gifts of rest and time: Rest in God's presence and take time to deepen your friendship with him. We are fortunate to have so many resources available to us to enrich our faith lives, including online spiritual guides, ancient prayer practices (*lectio divina*, the Rosary, novenas, litanies), and especially the sacraments. Attend adoration at your parish, join a rosary prayer group, sign up for parish retreats and book clubs. A resource that I recommend to friends who want to take their prayer lives to the next level is *The Better Part: A Christ-Centered Resource for Personal Prayer* by Fr. John Bartunek, which teaches you to meditate with Scripture and apply the Scripture passages to your own life.

When we lean on God, and he becomes our safe harbor, we find that he sometimes asks us to stop striving and simply be his child, loved and cherished because we are his and not because we do anything. Sometimes God asks us to nurture our own lives through reading, music, cooking, gardening, and other leisurely pleasures. Dr. Robert Royal reminds us, "Many things depend on us. But the greatest things, even the ability to carry out our duties, do not come merely by our own efforts. We have to invite graces that far exceed anything we ourselves could do."[1] This is true about every aspect of our journey through life, and it's certainly true as we carry on the mission of raising disciples. Transmitting faith to our children does not depend on us but upon God's grace. Yes, sometimes as we cooperate with his plan in evangelizing our children, there is indeed something for us to do; but often our job is to rest in God's care, spending time with him in prayer, worship, and study. We must tend the flame of our own faith if we want to share it with our children!

Accepting the Losses of Parenting

Just as our teens must face the void of adolescence and the losses that void brings, parents must face the losses that accompany raising teenagers. And what are these losses?

We have to let go of our image of our teens when they were small. Many parents feel an ache when their carefree, chubby-cheeked child seems to disappear overnight, replaced by somebody rather hairier and harder to read! Particular events can trigger the realization that our children are growing up and away from us. A friend of mine shared that on her son's eighth birthday, he suddenly seemed no longer a child, and she felt momentary grief. Think of Mary and Joseph when they lost Jesus (see Lk 2:41–52). They were traveling home from Jerusalem with a large caravan when they realized Jesus was not with their party, so they rushed back to Jerusalem to search for him. For three gut-wrenching days, they looked for him. Finally, they found him in a temple chatting with a group of adults. Like any mom, Mary told Jesus that he scared her half to death. But Jesus didn't seem scared. In fact, he asked Mary why she didn't know he would be in his Father's house. At this moment, Mary knew her little boy was growing up. It was time for her to begin letting him go; she needed to begin releasing him to his mission. So she took him home, and he was obedient to her, and she was obedient to God. Sometimes we must live with the unknowns of where God will lead our children when they outgrow our laps and stand up to walk away. My friend knew her eight-year-old was still a boy who needed his mommy for many years, but she recognized a shift in him physically and mentally — he seemed to be shooting up in stature and forward in confidence as a young man. Like Mary, she was called to adjust to this new stage in her mothering mission.

We also have to let go of our plans for our children when they make different plans. Most of us have dreams for our kids when they grow up, but during the teen years, it occasionally becomes clear that our teens' dreams for their lives are very different from ours! We can be blindsided when they make a decision that seems out of character, wrong for them, or misguided in some other way. Our future concert pianist announces he's become a full-time YouTuber, and we think he's lost his mind. Sometimes our assessment is correct, but at other times, our child just didn't share everything with us, or we imposed our own vision on him. Maybe he really hated the ten years of piano lessons and has no plans to touch another piano key ever again, let alone attend that fancy music school we picked out for him.

Our teens don't usually understand themselves much better than we do; they can be impulsive or attach to ideas and plans for the wrong reasons. I can't tell you how many times one of my teenagers said something, and a siren went off in my head. But after all my episodes of freaking out on these teenagers, I've learned that they often don't believe the things they're saying, and they're not really planning to do the things they're mulling over out loud to me. I'm not suggesting I shouldn't have said anything, but it was my tone that made matters worse. I over-corrected and over-reacted. So, take it from me: Don't panic. Satan uses fear against parents because he knows the turbulence of the teen years disorients many parents and gives them doubts about their kids and their own abilities to guide the rudder of the family ship. If your teen senses you are not in control, if he senses you think you're in over your head, it will make him insecure. In fact, some teenagers move into the dominant role with a parent when they sense the parent cannot care for them effectively; they take over and begin to direct the parent and the relationship. So even if you doubt yourself, in your relationship with your teen, remain as calm as possible and lead from a place of love, not fear.

The Great Wound: When Children Wander

One of the most difficult losses for a parent to bear is watching a child wander from the path of the true Faith. He might vocally reject the Church or simply disengage from any questions about God or religion. Whatever the reason, the wandering sheep hurts God more than us. Fortunately, God continues looking for our children even when they stop looking for him. In Matthew 18:12–14, Jesus tells his disciples:

> If a man has a hundred sheep, and one of them has gone astray, does he not leave the ninety-nine on the hills and go in search of the one that went astray? And if he finds it, truly, I say to you, he rejoices over it more than over the ninety-nine that never went astray. So, it is not the will of my Father who is in heaven that one of these little ones should perish.

This passage is simply astonishing. What shepherd would leave ninety-nine sheep to go after the one that can't seem to get with the program and follow the rest of the sheep? Our Lord does this. He is even more heartbroken than we are when our children lose their way; he knows better than we do what has been lost. Yet, he will not leave them or give up on them, and neither should we.

Not giving up doesn't mean we should cajole, threaten, or manipulate. While I'm confident that parents are correct to require their children and teens to continue participating in their family's faith practices and attending Mass, parents cannot orchestrate or require belief. Particularly when these children become adults, we cannot control their response to truth. For many reasons, some kids will reject the Church, and we cannot force their acceptance. In reality, God is the one who initiates the invitation of faith; he instills faith and virtue in our children, not us. He invites, he does not force; he leaves room for our child's response, even one of rejection. When this rejection seems stubborn, our role may be to back off while God continues extending that invitation. In these periods, we storm heaven with our prayers, and we entrust these children into the hands of our Blessed Mother. We never water down the truth, but we can be lavish with our love, nourishing the six roots of attachment, always welcoming these lost sheep with warmth.

Whether they have embarked on the discipleship path or

fallen into the brambles, the best way we can shepherd older teens and young adults is through the witness of our own faith lives. This isn't fluff and guff. I shared in chapter four this statement by Catholic sociologist Christian Smith:

> Parents exert far and away the greatest influence on their children's religious outcomes. ... The empirical evidence is clear. In almost every case, no other institution or program comes close to shaping youth religiously as their parents do — not religious congregations, youth groups, faith-based schools, missions and service trips, summer camps, Sunday school, youth ministers, or anything else. Those influences can reinforce the influence of parents, but almost never do they surpass or override it.[2]

Smith follows up by clarifying what parents can do to increase the likelihood that their kids will continue practicing their faith as adults. Smith said the first answer is for parents "simply to be themselves: believe and practice their own religion genuinely and faithfully. Children are not fooled by performances. They see reality. And when that reality is authentic and life-giving, they just may be attracted to something similar."[3] When we live our faith vibrantly, model joyful Christian living, and talk about what our faith means to us, we impact our children more than we realize. Sometimes we don't see the impact initially, but it shapes their perceptions and perhaps ultimately their receptivity to truth, goodness, and beauty.

Fluffing Your Nest

Finally, I want to give you some big-sisterly advice about taking care of yourself when your teenager eventually launches from your nest. Particularly when your child first launches off, you may experience a sense of mourning. Every time a child grows up and leaves home, it causes a seismic shift in our homes. Even when we still have other children at home, the dynamic and the space change dramatically.

Just as our teens have mixed feelings about growing up — they are ready to fly, but they know they will miss the protection and familiarity of home — we parents have mixed feelings too. Of course, we want to see our young adult children stretching toward their futures, but the deafening silence in their old bedrooms, the empty chair at the dinner table, the skimpier grocery bags are all reminders that our babies are gone.

Here's the thing: We are meant to be transformed through these times of change. God brings refreshment to us as we step into our new identity as parents of adult children. God reminds us, "Behold, I am doing a new thing; / now it springs forth, do you not perceive it? / I will make a way In the wilderness and rivers in the desert" (Is 43:19). He draws the curtain back and opens the window, and there we see the path forward. He is faithful! He reminds us of the things we loved before we were parents — hobbies, dreams, vocational longings — things we sacrificed to mother and father our small children. He leads us through new doors in service to the Church. He invites us to meet him in prayer in new ways, in new places, perhaps with new friends. We can have gratitude for what once was, but we must move forward because our mission is there. In prayer, express to God your honest sadness and fears as your child launches from the nest and ask him to reveal his dreams for you in this new stage of your life.

I've also discovered that when my children become adults, the relationships change, but they continue. Your relationship with your adult children will be delightful! I think I'm closer to my young adult son now than I was when he was a teenager. He shares articles with me, invites me to events, and likes to go out for tea and ice cream with me. He is currently trying to convince me to take a trip to Rome with him. My older daughter only recently launched from the nest, but I'm already delighting in watching her explore her independence and find her footing in her new college community. She sends me photos of her pet fish and her snack shelf, and I send her photos of her six birds making a mess in her bedroom. I find new ways to love my adult children as our relationship shifts, but often, when they need familiar comforts, I express my love through their old favorites — movies, food, traditions, nicknames — the small things that remind them of home.

So, when your child leaves home, your nest will change, but it will still need fluffing and feathering because it is still a home, still a sign of love. Your spouse and you (and perhaps younger children) still need your gifts of care and nurturance. Your younger children and even your adult children continue to need your shepherding; you will continue to be that devoted gardener tending the soil of faith in your home. Some of the details may change, but you still matter.

In this "Transform" section, we thought about the end of childhood and adolescence — the signs of maturity that we might see in our child as adulthood approaches and the purpose of this unique phase in our child's life. Adolescence is not like a starting stall in a horse race where our teen is waiting to start his journey through life. The teen years are a critical phase in a life well-lived. Adolescence is a time of testing. Our teen must confront difficult questions and doubts about his life, his purpose, and his faith in God. Our role is to facilitate the environment where our teen can wrestle safely through the crises of adolescence, so he is transformed and prepared for a life of discipleship. We are tested by adolescence, too. As disciple parents, we are transformed by God's care as he leads us through the shadows and valleys of our mission; we find ourselves refreshed by fresh pastures and still waters because God does not forget us (see Ps 23). By the grace of God, we are changed by the things we can't change.

Reflection and Direction

- How do you feel when you imagine your teen launching from your nest? Excited? Sad? Scared?
- All of these emotions at once? Know these mixed feelings are very common. Meditate on John 14:23–29. Rest in Christ's love as you ponder the changes ahead.

Are you worried about how your teen will handle his independence when he leaves home? Recall times in your life when things turned out better than you anticipated, times when you worried too much yet things turned out fine. How good God is! Even if your teen's launch doesn't go perfectly, he will probably do fine.

Conclusion
You're the Answer

I know well that the greater and more beautiful the work is,
the more terrible will be the storms that rage against it.
— St. Faustina Kowalska

Sometimes, accompanying teenagers on their journey to adulthood is like trying to catch a waterfall in a small bucket. Particularly in matters of faith and morals, we can feel we're drowning in the waterfall. Yet God knew what he was doing when he chose you to raise your particular teen. He always gives us what we need to accomplish our mission, especially for those tasks that seem beyond our capacity. In his mercy, God transforms doubts, fractures, and brokenness into something beautiful. When you doubt yourself as a disciple parent, cling to Christ's leg like a small child; he will scoop you up and walk for you. In one of life's great paradoxes, as we mature as Christian parents, we become more child-like. We let go, allowing ourselves to be led, becoming docile to God's lead, and what happens? We run into ourselves; we discover our true dignity and purpose.

For me, raising teenagers has been filled with surprises. I have been surprised by the power behind their feelings, the conviction in their opinions, and, yes, sometimes the stubbornness of their bad habits. I have been delightfully surprised by their compassion, their curiosity, and their heart for truth. I've also been surprised by how wrong my initial assumptions or predictions can be about my teens. This keeps me humble — and chuckling. Along with surprises, raising teenagers brings with it some mystery and ambiguity. If your experience is anything like mine, you will eventually wonder in retrospect at the way God guided and protected your teenager even when you didn't notice. He is drawing our teenagers closer to himself in ways we don't always understand, through instruments we don't appreciate.

Raising our children is a privilege. We get the front row seat as God draws a fascinating human being forward toward his or her destiny. While we all share a common dignity as children of God, we each have a singular purpose in God's plan for the world. God reveals our kids' purpose to them in unexpected ways in his own time. Watching this gorgeous unfolding in the lives of our children is one of the greatest blessings in our lives as parents.

If we're going to survive and thrive as disciple parents, we need to get comfortable with surprise, mystery, and ambiguity. We also need to let go of perfectionism. (We strive for perfection in virtue and holiness, but we are humble enough to know we will never be perfect this side of heaven.) You will make mistakes, as will your teen, and you will grow together through those mistakes. When you're disoriented as you wind your way through the parenting maze, or when you take a wrong turn, just turn around, and walk in a different direction. This is part of discipleship parenting: God parents you while you parent your teen. Give yourself some room to grow. Not only is it impossible to be a perfect parent, but you don't have to be perfect to raise great kids.

There is no perfect blueprint for evangelizing teenagers, but there is the right relationship: the parent-child bond. I began this book with the proposition that parents are the best answer to the crisis of faith retention in teens and young adults. I hope you believe it. Evangelizing teenagers begins where it ends: with love. And nobody loves your teen like you. God wired into you and your teen the dance of caring and dependence. Dance with your teen toward the feet of God. You don't need to have all the answers to your teen's faith struggles or questions; you need only *be* the answer to his deepest needs for love, safety, and belonging. Become the answer, and your teen will follow you as you nurture his budding faith. Through your generous love and protection, through your example and mentoring, eventually, your teen will be capable of taking the leap of faith and entering into a discipleship relationship with Christ.

Just as we don't need to be perfect to be disciple parents, our teens don't need to be perfect to become disciples. If we protect their hearts and stoke the flames of their faith, by the end of the teen years, they will be spiritually awake enough to respond to God's movements in their lives. Lead your teen confidently, inspire him to discover his mission, and give him the moral formation he needs to become a saint. With your shepherding, he will be prepared to embark on a life-long journey of transformation as a disciple of Christ. May God bless you and your teenager as you travel together in faith. I am praying for you!

— *On the feast of St. Faustina Kowalska*

Acknowledgments

I extend my sincere appreciation to …

The entire staff at OSV for your support and encouragement. I'm especially grateful to my editors Mary Beth Giltner and Rebecca Martin for sharing their gifts with me. Thank you for believing in this project and making it better than I envisioned.

Dr. Greg and Lisa Popçak, whose work helped me recognize that empathic, attachment-safe parenting was entirely compatible with my desire to be an authentic Catholic mother. You may never know this side of heaven the tremendous impact your work has had on the lives of ordinary Catholic families.

Dr. Gordon Neufeld, whose developmental paradigm helped me grow up as a mother. Your work has changed the lives of many and the futures of more.

The many teenagers in my life, including my language arts students, CCD students, and confirmands. You continually intrigue and inspire me, and your questions keep me on my toes.

My life is a beautiful schoolroom because of you.

My extended family, who always encouraged my passion for writing, especially my mom Lana, parents-in-law Ric and Barbara, sister Jeanelle, and sister-in-law Anita.

My husband Philip and children Aidan, Claire, Dominic, and Lydia for your patience and support, and especially your tolerance for too many pizzas and too few clean socks during the writing of this book!

Our Lady, Queen of Heaven, perfect Mother. *Totus Tuus.*

Notes

INTRODUCTION

1. See "The Sticky Faith Research" at https://fulleryouthinstitute
.org/stickyfaith/research.

2. David Bonagura presents the components of secularism and
the challenges they pose to Catholicism in his important book *Stead-
fast in Faith: Catholicism and the Challenges of Secularism* (Provi-
dence: Cluny Media, 2019).

3. John Paul II, *Fides et Ratio*, preface, vatican.va.

4. "It is the nature and quality of the relationship they have with
their child that is crucial — perhaps as much or more than what
parents do and teach religiously. Our study indicates that relationships with parents that are felt to be close, warm, and affirming are
associated with higher religious transmission than are relationships
perceived as cold, distant, or authoritarian — regardless of the level of
parental piety. This is particularly true for relations with fathers." Vern
Bengston, Norella M. Putney, and Susan Harris, *Families and Faith:
How Religion Is Passed Down across Generations* (New York: Oxford

University Press, 2013), 196.

5. One of the best studies on faith trajectory and the factors that most impact faith retention is the National Study of Youth and Religion (NYSR), analyzed in Christian Smith, *Young Catholic America: Emerging Adults In, out of, and Gone from the Church* (New York: Oxford University Press, 2014) .

6. One of the earliest Church Fathers, Saint Ignatius of Antioch (AD 35–107), was a disciple of the apostle John and one of the Church's first bishops. Ignatius warned early Christians against schism, the breaking away from the one true Church which Christ founded. He also wrote of the Eucharist: "There is one flesh of our Lord, Jesus Christ, and one cup of his blood that makes us one." This bishop asked for unity, obedience, and devotion to the Blessed Sacrament.

7. See Justin Martyr's account of the early liturgy (c. AD 155) in the *Catechism of the Catholic Church*, section 1345.

8. See Aidan Nichols, *The Holy Eucharist: From the New Testament to John Paul II* (Dublin: Veritas, 1991), chapters 1 and 2.

9. Eamon Duffy's *Stripping of the Altars* (New Haven: Yale University Press, 2005) provides a compelling correction to the view that the late-medieval Church was corrupt, empty, and unpopular. According to Duffy, the Reformation created a rupture for many common laypersons who relied on the traditions and beauty of Catholicism to sustain them in many ways.

10. Brandon's story of his conversion from atheism to Catholicism in *Why I Am Catholic* (Notre Dame: Ave Maria Press, 2017) presents separate chapters on these three premises and why they reasonably lead to the conclusion that the Church is the true faith. Accessible and highly recommended for curious teens and their parents.

CHAPTER 1:
Becoming Your Teen's Shepherd

1. John Westerhoff III, *Will Our Children Have Faith?* (New York:

Morehouse Publishing, 2012). Other well-regarded books on faith development across the lifespan include *Stages of Faith: The Psychology of Human Development and the Quest for Meaning* by James W. Fowler and *The Critical Journey: Stages in the Life of Faith* by Janet O. Hagberg and Robert A. Guelich.

2. Frank Mercadante, *Engaging a New Generation: A Vision for Reaching Catholic Teens* (Huntington, IN: Our Sunday Visitor, 2012), 74.

3. Westerhoff, 90.

4. Ibid., 94.

5. Ibid., 96.

6. Tim Clinton, *Attachments: Why You Love, Feel, and Act the Way You Do* (Brentwood, TN: Thomas Nelson Publishers, 2002), 36.

7. Gordon Neufeld, "How Children Are Meant to Attach" (recorded lecture, Neufeld Institute, *Intensive 1*, Session 11).

8. Pat Fagan, "The Synthesis Void in the Social Sciences," Marriage and Religion Research Institute, November 14, 2020, https://marri.us/the-synthesis-void-in-the-social-sciences.

9. Neufeld.

10. Gordon Neufeld, "Two Paths Diverge" (recorded lecture, Neufeld Institute, *Making Sense of Adolescence*, Session 2).

11. Neufeld.

12. John Paul II, *Catechesi Tradendae* (Catechesis in Our Times), vatican.va, par. 38.

13. Gordon Neufeld, "Walking through Aloneness and Sadness: The Necessary Road to Individuation" (recorded lecture, Neufeld Institute, *Making Sense of Adolescence*, Session 2).

14. See, for example, Angie McDonald et al., "Attachment to God and Parents: Testing the Correspondence vs. Compensation Hypothesis." *Journal of Psychology and Christianity* 24, no. 1 (2005): 21-28; Pehr Granqvist and Mario Mikulincer, "Religion as Attachment: Normative Processes and Individual Differences." *Personality and Social Psychology Review:* 14. https://doi.org/10.1177/1088868309348618.

15. Clinton, 148–154.

16. Joe Heschmeyer, *Who Am I, Lord? Finding Your Identity in Christ* (Huntington, IN: Our Sunday Visitor, 2020), 140.

17. See, for example, *Your Personality*: https://yourpersonality.net /attachment/.

18. See Dr. Neufeld's groundbreaking book *Hold On to Your Kids: Why Parents Need to Matter More Than Peers* (New York: Ballantine Books, 2006). See also his online seminars for counselors, teachers, and parents at the Neufeld Institute (neufeldinstitute.org).

19. The problem of peer orientation in the classroom and how effectively to reverse it are explored in *Reclaiming Our Students: Why Children Are More Anxious, Aggressive, and Shut Down Than Ever — And What We Can Do About It* by Hannah Beach and Tamara Neufeld Strijack (Vancouver: Page Two Books, 2020).

20. These shifting patterns in Western Europe and the United States are documented and explored in Michael Rutter and David J. Smith, eds., *Psychosocial Disorders in Young People: Time Trends and Their Causes* (Chichester: John Wiley & Sons, 1995).

21. Ibid., 168.

22. Ibid., 106.

CHAPTER 2:
Gaining Insight into Your Teen's Faith Journey

1. Here, Dr. Neufeld draws on classic attachment theory, including the work of John Bowlby and Harry Harlow.

2. "Liturgical catechesis aims to initiate people into the mystery of Christ (It is 'mystagogy.') by proceeding from the visible to the invisible, from the sign to the thing signified, from the 'sacraments' to the 'mysteries'" (CCC 1075).

3. https://onlineministries.creighton.edu/CollaborativeMinistry /Imagination/

4. "The Eucharist is 'the source and summit of the Christian life.' 'The other sacraments, and indeed all ecclesiastical ministries and

works of the apostolate, are bound up with the Eucharist and are oriented toward it. For in the blessed Eucharist is contained the whole spiritual good of the Church, namely Christ himself, our Pasch'" (CCC 1324).

5. Manuel Gonzalez Garcia, *The Bishop of the Abandoned Tabernacle*, ed. Sean Davidson, trans. Victoria G. Schneider (New York: Scepter, 2018), 38–39.

6. The streaming Catholic platform *Formed* (formed.org) has several films about the saints and biblical figures.

7. For example, Mk 1:15: "The time is fulfilled, and the kingdom of God is at hand; repent [Greek, *metanoeite*], and believe in the gospel"; Mk 6:11–12: "And if any place will not receive you and they refuse to hear you, when you leave, shake off the dust that is on your feet for a testimony against them. So they went out and preached that men should repent [Greek, *metanoosin*]."

8. This statement has been attributed to Bronfenbrenner for many years, but I can't locate the quote in his writing. For example, the statement is attributed to him in an article about him in a Cornell newpaper: Sharon Tregaskis, "50 years later, recalling a founder of Head Start," *Cornell Chronicle*, May 15, 2015, https://news.cornell.edu/stories/2015/05/50-years-later-recalling-founder-head-start.

9. Kara Powell, *The Sticky Faith Guide for Your Family* (Grand Rapids: Zondervan, 2014), 81–82. "A second theme in our interviews with fifty Sticky Faith parents was that they set firm walls around their time with their teenage children. … [They] keep their schedules free enough that they can dive into more informal, organic time together."

10. Ibid., 96.

11. Kim Cameron-Smith, *Discipleship Parenting: Planting the Seeds of Faith* (Huntington, IN: Our Sunday Visitor, 2020). In particular, see the sections "Emotions 101: Emotions and the Good Life" (pp. 107–112) and "Be an Emotion Coach" (pp. 157–167).

12. Ibid., 107.

13. Everything I know about these drives and their processes comes primarily from the lecture series I've taken through the
Neufeld Institute. In particular, in his series *Intensive 1: Making Sense
of Kids*, Dr. Neufeld does a tremendous job explaining to non-spe-
cialists the attachment, emergence, and integration drives. See https://
neufeldinstitute.org/course/neufeld-intensive-i-making-sense-of
-kids/.

14. Lisa Weiner, "The Two Essential Invitations," *Neufeld Institute
Editorials*, March 11, 2021, https://neufeldinstitute.org/the-two
-essential-invitations/.

15. John Paul II, "The Meaning of Man's General Solitude,"
vatican.va.

16. Ibid.

17. See, for example, Mk 1:35 and 5:16.

18. "If someone were to ask me what the liturgical life begins
with, I should answer: with learning stillness." Romano Guardini,
Preparing Yourself for Mass (New Hampshire: Sophia Institute Press,
1997), 11.

CHAPTER 3:
Anchoring Your Teen in Love and Faith

1. Professor James Pauley develops this point about invitation
and response in chapter nine of his book *An Evangelizing Catechesis:
Teaching from Your Encounter with Christ* (Huntington, IN: Our Sunday Visitor, 2020).

2. John Paul II, *FR, Preface*.

3. John Paul II, *Familiaris Consortio*, vatican.va, par. 42.

4. Ibid., par. 39.

5. Smith, 170–171.

6. "More than two million U.S. teens participate in mission trips
annually. While that's something to cheer, for five out of six of them,
the trips don't make a lasting mark on their lives." Powell, 184.

7. University of Michigan, "Empathy: College students don't have

as much as they used to, study finds," *Science Daily*, 29 May 2010, sciencedaily.com/releases/2010/05/100528081434.htm.

8. Paul J. Zak, *The Moral Molecule: The Source of Love and Prosperity* (New York: Dutton, 2012).

9. Gordon Neufeld, "The Natural Roots of Empathy," lecture delivered at the Neufeld Institute Conference 2021, April 17, 2021.

10. A free resource listing the seven principles or themes can be found at https://www.usccb.org/resources/themes-catholic-social-teaching. See also United States Conference of Catholic Bishops, *Compendium of the Social Doctrine of the Church* (Washington, D.C.: Libreria Editrice Vaticana, 2004). For teen-friendly guides, I like Catholic Central's videos and resources (https://www.catholiccentral.com/catholic-central-episodes/social-teaching) and *Foundations in Catholic Social Teaching: Living as a Disciple of Christ* (Ave Maria Press, 2015). I use these teen resources in my homeschooling and CCD classes.

11. Paul VI, *Gaudium et Spes*, vatican.va, par. 26. https://www.vatican.va/archive/hist_councils/ii_vatican_council/documents/vat-ii_const_19651207_gaudium-et-spes_en.html.

12. *Compendium of the Social Doctrine of the Church*, par. 301.

13. John Paul II, *Sollicitudo Rei Socialis*, vatican.va, par. 38.

14. Ibid., par. 34.

15. *Compendium of the Social Doctrine of the Church*, par. 571. The Magisterium of the Catholic Church aims to "educate the consciences of the faithful," but it "does not wish to exercise political power or eliminate the freedom of opinion of Catholics regarding contingent questions." So, for example, the option for the poor does not require Catholics to advocate for increased government programs.

CHAPTER 4:
Questing with Your Teen on Mission

1. The insights here are drawn partly from my private notes taken during Dr. Gordon Neufeld's lecture "The Natural Roots of Empathy" at the 2021 Neufeld Institute Conference.

2. Neufeld, *Hold On to Your Kids*, 256–258.

3. Ibid., 256–258.

4. Ibid., 258–261.

5. Powell, 96.

6. Kara Powell and Brad M. Griffin, *Sticky Faith Teen Curriculum: 10 Lessons to Nurture Faith Beyond High School* (Grand Rapids: Zondervan, 2011), 73.

7. Everett Fritz, *The Art of Forming Young Disciples: Why Youth Ministries Aren't Working and What to Do about It* (Manchester, NH: Sophia Institute Press, 2018), 59.

8. George Weigl, *Witness to Hope: The Biography of Pope John Paul II* (New York: Cliff Street Books, 1999), 60.

9. Christian Smith, "Keeping the Faith," *First Things*, May 2021, https://www.firstthings.com/article/2021/05/keeping-the-faith.

10. Code of Canon Law, c. 226, par. 2; c. 774, par. 2.

11. Mercadante, 129.

12. Ibid., 133.

CHAPTER 5:
Forging a Faith Village for Your Teen

1. Vinita Hampton Wright, "Finding God in Our Desires," *Ignatian Spirituality*, https://www.ignatianspirituality.com/finding-god-in-our-desires.

2. A great book to read with your teenager that addresses human desires and happiness is Dominick Albano's *The Fundamental Theory of Happiness: How to Find Your Purpose and Be More Joyful* (West Chester: Ascension Press, 2019). It's written at a level that teens and young adults can appreciate and understand.

3. If you're looking for resources to provide your teen with an overview of the Church's moral teaching, you might look at *Christian Morality: Our Response to God's Love* by Brian Singer-Towne (St. Mary's Press; www.SMP.org) or *Our Moral Life in Christ* by Peter Armenio (Midwest Theological Forum; www.theologicalforum.org).

Alternatively, you might enroll with your teen in an e-course like "Foundations: Life in Christ" at My Catholic Faith Delivered (www .mycatholicfaithdelivered.com) or Bishop Robert Barron's course "Seven Deadly Sins, Seven Lively Virtues" (www.wordonfire.org).

4. Some resources to help you navigate these tough issues with your teens: *Made This Way: How to Prepare Kids to Face Today's Tough Moral Issues* by Leila Miller and Trent Horn; *Tough Choices: Bringing Moral Issues Home* by Sean Lynch.

5. Cameron-Smith, 132.

6. Here I'm adapting some suggestions from catechist Jared Dees in "Reflections on Developing Virtues in Teens," *The Religion Teacher*, https://www.thereligionteacher.com/a-reflection-on-developing -virtues-in-teens/.

7. For more family read-aloud ideas, see my articles at osvnews .com and kimcameronsmith.com.

8. Killian J. Healy, *Awakening Your Soul to the Presence of God: How to Walk with Him Daily and Dwell in Friendship with Him Forever* (New Hampshire: Sophia Institute Press, 1999), 54–58.

9. Most of my handouts are available free on my website: kimcameronsmith.com. If you're looking for more of Fr. Mike's decision-making advice, he has two books on the topic: *Pray, Decide, and Don't Worry: 5 Steps to Discerning God's Will* (West Chester: Ascension Press, 2019) and *How to Make Great Decisions* (Palm Beach: Wellspring, 2019).

10. "This openness to God, without which discernment cannot be made, cannot be taken for granted. In fact, in his Spiritual Exercises, Ignatius prepares us for discernment primarily through the quest for this openness." Timothy M. Gallagher, O.M.V., *Discerning the Will of God: The Ignatian Guide to Christian Decision Making* (New York: The Crossroads Publishing Company, 2009), 33.

11. Dogmatic Constitution on Divine Revelation, *Dei Verbum*, vatican.va, par. 21.

12. Available at kimcameronsmith.com.

13. Of course, God can communicate with his children in any manner he wants and in any manner that we need. God spoke to both Moses and Elijah on Mount Sinai: Moses heard God's voice in thunder while Elijah heard it in quiet. Elijah looked for God's voice in the thunder, but it wasn't there. (Compare Ex 19:16–19 to 1 Kgs 19:11–13.) God chose the means of his communication in both cases. So, God can communicate with our teens through noise, but my concern here is that our teens often use noise to avoid themselves, God, and life. If they are seeking God, God will reveal himself to them.

14. He warns, though, that not all prayer feels life-giving; sometimes we experience desolation in prayer.

15. See Laurence Murphy, SJ, "Psychological Problems of Christian Choice," *The Way Supplement* 24 (1975): 26-35, accessed online at https://www.theway.org.uk/Back/s024Murphy.pdf.

16. Carolyn Parkinson, Adam M. Kleinbaum, and Thalia Wheatley, "Similar neural responses predict friendship," *Nature Communications 9,* 332 (2018), https://doi.org/10.1038/s41467-017-02722-7.

17. "Risk-averse teens sway peers to make safer choices," *Science Daily*, November 30, 2020, www.sciencedaily.com /releases/2020/11/201130150316.htm.

18. From the Office of Readings for the Feast of Saints Basil the Great and Gregory Nazianzen, January 2.

CHAPTER 6:
Mentoring Your Teen in Discernment

1. In particular, see the section "Emotions 101: Emotions and the Good Life" (pp. 107–112).

2. Adele Faber and Elaine Mazlish, *How to Talk So Teens Will Listen and Listen So Teens Will Talk* (New York: Harper Collins, 2006), 12–13.

3. Louis Bouyer, *Eucharist: Theology and Spirituality of the Eucharistic Prayer*, trans. Charles Quinn (Notre Dame, Indiana: University of Notre Dame Press, 1968), 114–115, discussing the connection

between the Eucharist and the martyrdom of Saint Polycarp. See also CCC 1323.

4. John Paul II, *FC*, par. 11.

5. Robert E. Rector, Kirk A. Johnson, and Lauren R. Noyes, "Sexually Active Teenagers Are More Likely to Be Depressed and to Attempt Suicide: A Report of the Heritage Center for Data Analysis," *The Heritage Foundation*, June 3, 2003, https://files.eric.ed.gov/fulltext /ED476392.pdf.

6. Edward O. Laumann et al., *The Social Organization of Sexuality: Sexual Practices in the United States* (Chicago: University of Chicago Press, 1996), 503.

7. Gordon Neufeld, "The Sexualization of Attachment: The Design" (recorded lecture, Neufeld Institute, *Adolescence and Sexuality*, Session 1).

8. Ibid.

9. Gordon Neufeld, "Adolescent Sexuality and Vulnerability" (recorded lecture, Neufeld Institute, *Adolescence and Sexuality*, Session 3).

10. Gordon Neufeld, "Sexualization of Attachment: The Deviations" (recorded lecture, Neufeld Institute, *Adolescence and Sexuality*, Session 2).

11. Paul VI, *Humanae Vitae*, vatican.va, par. 12; CCC 2363.

12. "How Planned Parenthood Teaches Sex Education," *Planned Parenthood Action Fund*, https://www.plannedparenthoodaction.org /issues/sex-education/how-planned-parenthood-teaches-sex -education.

13. The Pontifical Council for the Family, *The Truth and Meaning of Human Sexuality: Guidelines for Education within the Family*, vatican.va, par. 43, emphasis mine.

14. The Pontifical Council for the Family, par. 44.

CHAPTER 7:
Managing Challenges While
Protecting Your Relationship

1. The age of majority is 19 in Nebraska and Alabama and 21 in Mississippi.

2. Edward Sri, "In the Dust of the Rabbi: Clarifying Discipleship for Faith Formation Today," *The Catechetical Review* (January-March 2018), 10.

3. "As we have already said, creation is a gift to man. His fullness and deepest dimension is determined by grace, that is, by participation in the interior life of God himself, in his holiness. This is also, in man, the interior foundation and source of his original innocence." John Paul II, General Audience, January 30, 1980, vatican.va, par. 3.

4. Neufeld, *Hold On to Your Kids*, 111.

5. Ibid., 111.

6. Ellen Hendriksen, PhD, "Failure to Launch Syndrome," *Scientific American*, May 18, 2019, https://www.scientificamerican.com/article/failure-to-launch-syndrome.

7. Jason Craig, *Leaving Boyhood Behind: Reclaiming Catholic Brotherhood* (Huntington, IN: Our Sunday Visitor, 2019), 23.

8. Craig, 24.

9. Neufeld, *Hold On to Your Kids*, 111.

10. Jason Craig's *Leaving Boyhood Behind* provides many helpful ideas for recovering rites of passage that work for boys under the guidance of men. He encourages men to help boys forge a sense of brotherhood with other men through a culture of heroic virtue, discipline, and masculinity oriented toward fatherhood.

11. Arnold van Gennep, *The Rites of Passage*, 2nd ed. (Chicago: University of Chicago Press, 2019).

12. https://www.quinceanera-boutique.com/quinceanera-tradition/.

13. Gordon Neufeld, "The Attachment Factor" (recorded lecture, Neufeld Institute, *Intensive 1*, Session 10). One of Gordon Neufeld's

crucial insights is that facing separation is our preeminent threat as humans. The threat evokes specific emotional responses: alarm, frustration, pursuit. No human being can bear too much separation without the triggering of defenses. These defenses are meant to protect us, but if they become stuck, they can become features of our personalities, leading to relationship issues. Dr. Neufeld also teaches a fifteen-session lecture series focusing on the separation complex: https://neufeldinstitute.org/course/neufeld-intensive-ii-the-separation-complex/.

14. As an aside, I think there's an argument to be made for returning to the former practice of confirming kids before high school. High schoolers need the outpouring of the Holy Spirit and the graces received in confirmation now more than ever! My family switched parishes a few years ago, partly so that our two younger children could go through confirmation preparation in middle school; children are confirmed in eighth grade in our new parish.

15. Eli Hecht, "How to Prepare a Boy for Bar Mitzvah," *Chabad of South Bay*, https://www.chabadsb.org/templates/articlecco_cdo/aid/59988/jewish/How-to-Prepare-a-Boy-for-Bar-Mitzvah.htm.

16. In fact, confirmation is a sacrament of *martyrdom*. (This might be too dramatic a detail for some of our teens, but others will think it's pretty awesome.) In the Old Testament, a community laid hands on somebody because they were being set apart — not for admiration, but for death and for sacrifice. When the apostles received the Holy Spirit at Pentecost, they were empowered not only to evangelize, but to become martyrs. Every apostle except John was martyred for the Faith. Jesus knows we don't have the strength to endure suffering for his sake, so through the power of the Holy Spirit, he gives us what we need to accomplish it.

17. Sri, "In the Dust of the Rabbi," 11.

CHAPTER 8:
Toward Owned Faith

1. Robert Royal, "Summer Stillness," *The Catholic Thing*, August 9, 2021, https://www.thecatholicthing.org/2021/08/09/summer-stillness/.

2. Smith, "Keeping the Faith" https://www.firstthings.com /article/2021/05/keeping-the-faith.

3. Ibid.

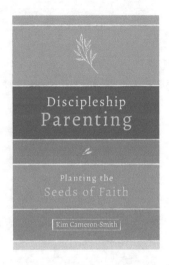